lism

Concepts in the Social Sciences

Series Editor: Frank Parkin

Published Titles

Concepts in the Social Sciences

Pluralism

Gregor McLennan

Open University Press
Buckingham

Open University Press
Celtic Court
22 Ballmoor
Buckingham
MK18 1XW

First published 1995

A catalogue record of this book is available from the British Library

ISBN 0 335 19154 1 (pb)   0 335 19155 X (hb)

Typeset by Type Study, Scarborough
Printed in Great Britain by J. W. Arrowsmith Ltd, Bristol

For Suzanne, Ruairidh and Finn
with all my love and thanks

Contents

Preface

Not so long ago within the social sciences, and in particular in the teaching of basic sociology and political science, the term pluralism mainly designated one particular school of thought and scholarship: that of American 'empirical democratic theory' of the 1950s to the early 1970s. There is no doubt that this particular pluralist current is still worthy of study today, and indeed a number of valuable debates about the achievement and legacy of what can be called 'conventional pluralism' or 'political science pluralism' have occurred since that time. Yet there are a number of past and present currents of thought which also qualify for the label 'pluralism', and these currents depart, sometimes significantly, from the conventional pluralist model of society and politics. One aim of this book is to reorient us into seeing pluralism as signalling, appropriately, a *plurality* of interpretative perspectives rather than just one. Pluralists have been around for quite a while, and they come in many varieties.

A related aim is to fulfil the brief given in the general title of the series in which this text appears. Pluralism today is probably best regarded not so much as a particular school of thought or coherent body of theory – a proper 'ism', so to speak. Rather, pluralism can be viewed as a key concept in the social sciences. As such it signals a series of meanings, problems and preferences which can be found or built into a range of otherwise very different theories and theoretical interests. Pluralism is in that sense a 'modal' concept and not a substantive 'end point' doctrine; essentially, it indicates our acknowledgement of multiplicity and difference across and within particular social fields or discourses.

I further contend that, like many key concepts of this sort in the social sciences, the very articulation of what pluralism stands for necessarily involves the invocation of its conceptual opposite or 'boundary condition', namely, a sense of unity and integration; the insistence that multiplicity must end somewhere if theoretical intelligibility and political strategy are to be possible at all. Across a number of levels of analysis – methodological, social, political – some basic and taxing issues are generated by the dialectical interplay between pluralistic dispersion and integrative or 'monistic' unification, and it is these issues that I explore. Overall, I argue that, viewed as a modal concept, pluralism is an indispensable and ever-interesting reference point across a range of social scientific debates and research specialisms. However, I find it important to add that the assertion of pluralism in any particular field does not in and of itself usually produce any clear *solutions* to long-standing political and analytical concerns. The hope that appears to be increasingly being invested in generalized pluralism as a way forward in critical social theory today may be misplaced to that extent.

Introduction: Pluralism Revived

I

During the 1970s, when many critical social scientists enthusi-astically aspired to be both scientific and politically radical, 'pluralism' was a considered term of abuse. The best known variant of pluralism was, and probably remains, the (mainly American) political science tradition of 'empirical democratic theory', and this corpus of work was frequently designated pejoratively as being both ideologically conservative and theoretically 'functionalist'. As expressed in its key texts of the 1950s and 1960s, American pluralism was taken by many radicals as representing little more than an apology for corporate capitalism, a western Cold War ideology parading as mature social science. The term pluralism was used in looser ways too, indicating not so much an analytical model of the political process as a more general intellectual orientation. Thus, according to the ascendant (structuralist, neo-Marxist) norms of the 70s, it was often thought that to be a pluralist in the academic disciplines of sociology and politics generally meant:

- being concerned with superficial, contingent behaviour rather than pervasive and enduring social structures;
- being 'merely' descriptive rather than rigorously theoretical in style and ambition;
- lacking a coherent organizing 'paradigm' to guide one's academic work.

More loosely still, pluralism indicated a certain type of temper-ament, a particular psycho-personal frame of mind. In this sense, 'pluralism' is not significantly different from the general gist of 'liberalism', an equally unpopular state of intellectual being for radicals of the 70s stamp. Taken that way, pluralism as an outlook on life and politics could be expected to appeal to the overly-tolerant, *pseudo*-tolerant, ostensibly humanistic, and intellectually eclectic sort of person; the sort of person who does not really have clear opinions on anything; the well-meaning type who, deep down, does not fundamentally want to question or change society; the faint-hearted ones, hesitant even about pushing academic sociology or political science to their full critical potential; the sort of people who fiddle while Rome burns.

That sketch, of course, is impressionistic. I think it is important, however, to begin our journey into pluralism by conveying something of the affective resonance of the term in the period from the late 1960s through to the mid-1980s. This is partly because that cartoon character of pluralism did appear in a wide range of social science courses and textbooks, and the prevailing attitude was negative; as a world view, whilst pluralism was probably 'better' than outright neo-liberal individualism, it certainly lacked clarity, depth and commitment by comparison with both 'straight' neo-liberalism and with the preferred radical-structural alternatives. Since that time, however, there has been a rather dramatic sea change in the prevailing attitude towards pluralism, taken both as a specific tradition of political analysis and as a general intellectual orientation. True, you seldom find critical social scientists today openly revoking the earlier negative consensus on 'apologetic' pluralism. Nevertheless, pluralism is nowadays part of the 'structure of feeling' of the critical wing of western intellectual culture to a degree that would have been unthinkable even 10 or 15 years ago.

Today, in the mid-1990s, declarations of pluralism come from many quarters. Some represent the revenge of 'bourgeois' political science over Marxism, in the light of the waning of class as a political predictor and in the light of the pluralization of the former state socialist societies. Some represent, in philosophy and sociology, the 'anti-foundationalism' that is emphasized in various poststructuralist and postmodernist discourses, according to which the very goal of unity and coherence in politics and theory is searchingly put into question. In such contemporary usages, pluralism indicates amongst other things: a suitably humble and relativistic acceptance that there is a range of cultural values; opposition to all forms of cultural imperialism; release from the dead hands of Enlightenment scientism and rationalism; fruitful methodological diversity; endorsement of different ways of knowing and of being; creativity and openness in theory; the embrace of a wide range of social interests and interest groups in the modern political scene, none of which are 'primary' in any demonstrable sense; affirmation of democracy as an end in itself; attention to the complexities of political allegiance; the sense that our social and political identities are now chosen rather than inherited; anti-utopian political horizons; enshrinement of the principle of 'equal but different'.

Amongst this intriguing batch of new-style pluralist elements, some definitely overlap with old-style political pluralism, whilst others look quite fresh. At the very least, there is something about the phraseology, the discursive framing, of contemporary pluralism which seems to set it apart from previous mind-sets. But does that discursive freshness really reflect a substantively different type of pluralism or not? Is pluralism today a matter of old wine in new bottles or not? This is an important question which is not easy to duck. A born-again liberal pluralist might be inclined to say that with the ascendancy of the new pluralism, the undeserved eclipse of conventional pluralism by radical theory in the 1970s has at last, and decisively, been set to rights. One of today's radical pluralists on the other hand might in response insist on the point that since the assumptions of *both* old-style liberal and old-style Marxist thought alike have been definitively overturned, the new pluralism must be viewed as being completely unlike previous incarnations of pluralism.

II

This book contains resources which will assist readers to make up their own minds on the interesting and politically consequential issue of whether or not the new pluralism is really new. I would also want to register some caution about getting too carried away with this aspect of our topic, however. For one thing, a considerable effort of basic clarification and analysis is required before open polemicizing is likely to be useful. Second, intelligent answers to questions like 'does the new pluralism simply replay the old pluralism?' often depend very much on which particular author or issue is under examination. An indiscriminate 'yes' or 'no' approach is therefore not likely to be very interesting in that regard. Thus, for example, before setting up a new paradigm clash between old and new, conservative and radical pluralisms, we might do well to recall that Robert A. Dahl was widely regarded by 70s critics as the doyen of conventional political pluralist theory. Yet Dahl's work even back in the early 50s probably *least* matched up to the potted version of liberal pluralism which found its way into the textbooks. We might note also that conventional pluralism experienced its own internal transformation into something a little more radical during the later 1970s.[1]

Third, your views on the 'old versus the new' issue will depend greatly on what kind of beast you think a 'theory' is. It has to be said that there is a considerable degree of (stimulating) confusion in the social sciences today about what our concepts and theories are actually meant to do for us.[2] The main options are as follows. If you regard theory as the business of amassing propositional truths which tell us more and more about social reality 'out there', then you may indeed be inclined to see the new, postmodernist variant of pluralism as merely terminological window-dressing. It's all been said before, you might want to think. You might then want to take some critical pleasure in the apparent irony that some of the very same concepts that once did service for the liberal western way of life are now being summoned up in the service of radical alternatives to liberalism. There is undoubtedly some mileage in this 'Platonist' view of theories, especially in view of the rather shallow tendency amongst some theoretical commentators to declare old models and resources to be utterly discredited and utterly superseded whenever a promising new idea comes along.

Even so, the Platonist theoretical temperament has been forcefully challenged by writers who have ceased to regard theoretical endeavour as being *representational* in character. That is to say, rather than treat theories as 'windows on the world', they should perhaps be treated more as 'vocabularies of insight'. In this idiom, theories have no special verisimilitude, no direct power to 'represent' reality as it really is. Instead, theories must be reconceived as comprising various statements, metaphors and intellectual tactics which are meaningful only in the light of their specific discursive and historical formation. Rather than being seen as mirrors, pictures or proofs, theories are ways of getting people talking and engaging, and they work on the imagination rather than on 'the facts', offering 'insight' rather than 'sight'. From this standpoint, the new-found utility of pluralist concerns and concepts, and their reworking within a vocabulary of radical democratic postmodernism, is precisely what is interesting. The thinking here is that significantly new insights on pluralism *can* readily be generated through 'merely' rhetorical realignment. Indeed, that is probably the way that all social theory develops.

I do not propose to resolve this metatheoretical issue here. I only want to indicate that it is very much a 'live' issue which has consequences for our various debates on pluralism. Along with many Platonists, I feel that theories *are* to be judged, in part and indirectly no doubt, by their truth-telling and reality-representing capacities. So I also hold that there is some critical purchase in drawing attention to the ironies of the postmodernist recycling of earlier liberal pluralist themes. At the same time, it is probably a little boring to seek to equate liberal and postmodern pluralist orientations in an 'I told you so' fashion. The differences in context, theoretical inflection and political resonance are sufficient, at the very least, to explore with interest the significance of the label's new lease of life.

To that end, we need to reactivate our sensitivity to the various possible meanings and implications of pluralism, and this is one primary task undertaken in this book. I therefore attempt to convey a sense of the richness and variety of pluralist concerns over the years, drawing particular attention to the way in which pluralism has once again become a seemingly progressive, radical position in social thought. A major claim I want to make in this regard is that it is pluralism that lies at the heart of much of what is tangible and valuable in postmodernist social theory. This is an observation that has had little sustained elaboration so far, but as one commentator has nicely put it:

> The vocabulary of pluralism has become standard fare in the postmodernist literature, used to flag the plurality of signifiers and signifieds, the plurality of language-games, the plurality of narratives, and the plurality of social practices. Plurality, it is attested, infiltrates our grammar, our concept formation, our social attitudes, our principles of justice, and our institutions. Veritably, plurality appears to have become a global phenomenon of postmodern life.[3]

I want to endorse this insight, and furthermore to tackle a major auxiliary issue: even assuming that the postmodern condition is characterized in various ways by an emphasis on plural*ity*, does this entail that a coherent and convincing plural*ist* programme for theory and politics is now available?

In pursuing this matter, I will be showing that the very concept of pluralism is a peculiarly elusive and knotty one. It is possible, for example, to be a theoretically 'radical' or 'moderate' pluralist. Also, you can be a pluralist of the 'Left' or a pluralist of the 'Right'. You can be a pluralist right across the fields of ontology, epistemology, methodology, social theory, morality, politics and culture, or you can be a pluralist, if you like, in just one or two of these domains.

Another commentator states baldly that 'pluralism is currently one of those values to which everybody refers but whose meaning is unclear and far from adequately theorised',[4] and from what I have just said, it is easy to see why. I think that the situation is improving, however, and the second goal of this book is to further that process of clarification and assessment. In that regard, I find it useful to distinguish between three broad levels of pluralism: methodological pluralism, sociocultural pluralism, and political pluralism.[5] Let me trail what is involved in each of these sub-divisions.

Methodological pluralism refers to philosophical and interpretative problems in assessing diverse claims to knowledge about the social world. Methodological pluralism posits the existence and validity of:

- a multiplicity of appropriate research methods;
- a multiplicity of substantive interpretative 'paradigms';
- many truths;
- many worlds.

We will see in due course what each of these pluralist commitments involves, but for the moment we just need to dwell on the interesting shifts of emphases across these four placards.

Similarly, *sociocultural* pluralism requires adherence to one, or (on a more stringent basis) all, of the claims that there are:

- many types of important social relations;
- many subcultures;
- multiple identities;
- multiple selves.

Finally, *political* pluralism comes in different strengths and stresses too, offering a scale of commitment to diversity in the polity:

- recognition of sociocultural difference;
- facilitation of difference;
- representation of difference in all basic decision-making arrangements.

III

The third main aspect of my study is to engage in a critical evaluation of pluralism(s). As with all the 'isms' which carry significant political implications, pluralism is a decidedly – maddeningly – 'multi-accentual' and 'essentially contested' term. Its constitutive vagueness, in other words, forms part of its ideological flexibility, so that it is eminently capable of signifying reactionary things in one phase of debate but progressive things in the next. But these discursive connotations of pluralism, its cultural 'vibes' as it were, are nowadays once again swinging sharply away from the negative to the positive, and it is important, I feel, to try in that context to keep some critical distance from the dominant affective resonance. I do not mean to somehow prevent us being pluralists, if that is what our convictions dictate. I do think, however, that social scientists are obliged to subject all theoretical and political options to serious scrutiny, perhaps especially if an outlook is shaping up as the prevailing academic/ideological view. The impression is sometimes given out today, for example, that all things plural, diverse and open-ended are to be automatically regarded as 'good', and that all things single, closed and uniform are correspondingly 'bad'. But in my view these equations need to be questioned and held at a distance, if only because the cultural and political climate might once again change in due course, reversing once again those apparently 'natural' assumptions. Things may look very different in 2030. If what is 'critical' about social science theory is its tendency to undermine the orthodoxies of both common sense and the academy, then we need to fix upon the blind spots and limitations of pluralism today.

I particularly want to remind us of the considerable *dilemmas* that perennially confront any assertion of pluralism as a principled position.[6] Notably – notoriously – there is the issue of 'where to draw the line'. Pluralism stands for diversity in politics and methodology, but is there not a point at which healthy diversity turns into unhealthy dissonance? Does pluralism mean that 'anything goes'? If it does not, then what exactly *are* the criteria for calling a halt to the potentially endless multiplication of valid ideas, cultures, and political groups? Despite the fact that pluralists are not usually theoretical or political nihilists in the strict sense, typically the terms by which pluralism is asserted – especially in postmodernist forms of pluralism – leave little scope for imposing rational limits on entry into the pluralist republic.

My three overall objectives are, then: to give a sense of the *diversity* of pluralist traditions, to analyse the *different levels and meanings* of pluralism as a concept, and to articulate the *problems* pluralism faces as well as the advantages it offers as a synthetic perspective for critical theory and politics. In the following chapter, I show the centrality of issues of pluralism to present debates by focusing on just one important discourse of theory and politics, namely feminism. Chapters 3 and 4 widen the lens to describe some of the other main intellectual contexts of discussion in which pluralist ideas have been prominent. The following two chapters then look more closely at different aspects or 'levels' of pluralism – methodological, sociocultural and political – indicating their typical characteristics, interconnections, and difficulties.

In Chapter 7 I rehearse the main themes and arguments in the book, in the form of some summary theses. Overall, pluralism is not only a rich vein of social scientific thinking, it is a telling and appropriate expression of our intellectual and moral condition in the 1990s. Pluralism also offers fertile ground for pursuing nonsectarian and hopeful goals in theory and practice. Indeed, in some ways, there is probably no option today but to be a pluralist of sorts. However, the problems facing any strong articulation of pluralism are very considerable, and I will be arguing as a consequence that formal expressions of pluralism in themselves by no means constitute a satisfactory rationale, either for the human sciences, or for radical democratic politics.

Feminism, Pluralism and Postmodernism

I

Feminism today has achieved very considerable legitimacy within the critical human sciences, a legitimacy that has been hard won by challenging the theories, scholarly norms and career practices which have worked intellectually to marginalize women. There is little doubt that conventional pluralist political science fits very well the idea of a male bastion in that sense. As a professional subculture, ostensibly committed to the empirical method and taking the game of political negotiation pretty much as it found it, conventional pluralism was not very amenable to the sort of ultimate questioning, politicized research culture and subcultural disturbance that has accompanied the feminist intellectual revolution. Substantively, too, whilst in principle feminism could no doubt be 'added on' to the pressure group spectrum often described by pluralists, women's politics were certainly not amongst their favoured examples of interest intermediation, and in any case feminism itself would most likely only count as one group interest amongst many others. Consequently, the very idea of a holistic theory of pervasive gender oppression such as motivated 1970s feminism runs entirely against the grain of conventional pluralism. Correspondingly, to this day, references in the feminist literature to pluralism of the 'political science' sort tend to be sharply dismissive.

Increasingly, however, that story of the relationship between feminism and pluralism is of limited value. For one thing, as already noted, the conventional pluralist tradition took a markedly more critical turn through the 1970s and 1980s. In parallel, feminists have for their part come to question whether '1970s feminism' remains a viable theoretical or political project. Moreover, the powerful feminist critique of established social science, including familiar alternatives to pluralism (such as Marxism), has involved some distinctly pluralistic elements. Finally, of all the various contexts in which postmodernist themes are debated, it is arguably within feminist debate that questions of methodological, social and political pluralism emerge as being at the heart of what is interesting and disruptive about postmodernism itself. Approaching the current standing of pluralism through feminist debates thus gives us a useful single focus of analysis for the dimensions of theoretical appraisal that will be considered further in subsequent chapters.

II

Let me first sketch the elements of a theoretically 'monistic' world view, particularly one which seeks to be socially and politically emancipatory. To laypeople, it often seems strange that perspectives which claim to want to help and encourage ordinary people to change their lives in revolutionary ways typically develop highly abstract and philosophical discourses. Ironically of course, this feature of revolutionary thought serves in some ways to hinder its easy translation into popular action. Yet, on reflection, it is obvious why revolutionary doctrines must couch the language of action in abstract terms, and why, lying behind every form of radical politics, sits a distinctive and primary epistemology. Simply put, the collective realization of a wholly different way of *being* requires each of us to perceive the emancipatory promise of a wholly different way of *knowing*. To fulfil this promise, extensive critical engagement with orthodox knowledges and orthodox theories of knowledge is unavoidable and appropriate. The revolutionary alternative is thus required to effect real change via an apparent 'detour' into the realm of philosophy. Necessarily, a distinctive and emancipatory politics requires a different account of, and appeal to, the knowing, experiencing and acting subject. Only if a 'new subject' is coherently envisaged and theoretically justified can a qualitatively new political order emerge.

In this type of monistic discourse, an unbreakable unity of theory and practice is typically asserted, running all the way down from epistemological and metaphysical considerations to specific policy proposals. In that tightly integrated world-view, the social may well be accepted as being complex and variegated, but essentially its workings – and any feasible alternative to those workings – must be analysable according to one singular and primary logic above all others. Theories which do not correspond to the favoured vision can then be characterized as being seriously flawed or ideological in some way, and political positions which derive from these flawed ideologies, or which appear to have no deep grounding at all, can be classified as both incorrect and harmful.

For many feminists today, partly under the influence of postmodernist currents, this kind of monistic logic has fallen right out of favour, and yet its elements can be clearly witnessed in the structure of what is often now frequently referred to as '1970s western feminism'. The individualism and empiricism and simple male-centredness of the liberal academic tradition cast a stigma of 'bias' on politicized research which aimed to rescue the women who had been collectively hidden from history. Marxism of course provided a ready made 'collectivist' and 'activist' alternative to liberalism, but the primary category of *class* in Marxist analysis was felt by many feminists to render invisible the gendered nature of production and reproduction in the social economy. To that extent Marxism itself was felt to be conniving in the exclusion of women from the sphere of public political activity, and consequently from social theory too.

On the epistemological plane, the ruling tradition and its official opposition seemed to share in common the belief that knowledge could be wholly disinterested and objective. Both assumed that once the one truly objective theory of society could be found, the social world could be controlled and 'mastered' in much the same way as the physical world was being mastered in the development of the natural sciences. In response to this orthodox storyline, feminism registered an incisive epistemological critique: the very presuppositions of mastery and instrumentalism, which so often down the centuries have been invoked in depictions of the nature and purpose of disinterested objectivity, are really little more than the reflection of specifically *male* social practices and ideologies. Lofty disinterestedness reflects the possibility of thought without commitment, of legislating for human knowledge from a privileged base and without ties or responsibilities. Indeed, 'mastery' of nature/society is probably the tallest of boy's own stories, a story of conquest and penetration, a tying up of inconvenient loose ends and hangers on. This parallel between scientific philosophy and men's invasive attitudes to women, and the insight that even – especially – in the hallowed sphere of philosophical reflection men conceive of their emotional attachments and domestic responsibilities as 'merely contingent', set the scene for an extensive effort to articulate a specifically feminist theory of knowledge. This 'feminist standpoint' epistemology would be rooted firmly in women's experience, and would be decidedly more collective, interactive, provisional and nurturing in character than the traditional paradigms of empiricism, rationalism or dialectical materialism.

In this way, a comprehensive paradigm of feminist theory and practice was established, in which a coherent political cause was grounded in considerations of epistemology and general social theory. At each level of analysis, the feminist perspective is sharply distinguished from the academic and political 'malestream'.

From the start it must be pointed out that many feminists were uncomfortable with a monistic expression of feminism, and with its resulting political sectarianism. Notably, there have been many attempts to generate a synthesis between Marxism and feminism. A notable defender of 'feminism unmodified' however, Catharine MacKinnon, shows how, once feminism is in place as a totalizing perspective, such attempts at synthesis involve impossible compromises. MacKinnon argues that feminist concepts and goals simply cannot be merged with those of other theories and movements, such as Marxism. This is because Marxism and feminism

> do not mean to exist side by side, pluralistically ... they exist to argue, respectively, that the relations in which many work and few gain, in which some dominate and others are subordinated, in which some fuck and others get fucked and everyone knows what those words mean, are the prime moment in politics.[1]

MacKinnon goes on: 'Attempts to create a synthesis between marxism and feminism, termed socialist–feminism, have recognized neither the separate integrity of each theory nor the depth of antagonism between them'.[2] The implication here is that coherent theories go all the way down, that they are exclusive and seamless. It is not that Marxism, for example, is unworthy of allegiance or lacking in powerful analytical and political resources; it is simply that if you are a feminist, those goals and resources cannot be yours. Indeed, as a feminist, which definitively means allegiance to the view that sexual exploitation is the key to both understanding and changing the social world, you are necessarily committed to relegating all other coherent and plausible theories to a secondary position.

Taking something of this argument on board, further attempts were made, if not to merge, then perhaps at least to articulate connections between class and gender as social coordinates. At least in terms of MacKinnon's analysis, however, the very project of this type of 'dual systems' theory is manifestly paradoxical. For it would seem that explicitly to conceive of society along the lines of two separate logics (sex/gender and class), which interlock here and there, is to assume from the outset that the question of analytical and political primacy cannot be established. In that case, perhaps we can imagine just *one* system, composed of the analytically separable elements of gender and class? However, that solution too somehow only manages to place sex/gender alongside an *already existing* central reference point, namely class. This inevitably has the discursive effect of rendering feminist theory less than fully revolutionary, and in that sense once again feminist political concerns appear to be subordinated to, or incorporable within, those of conventional class politics.

From that sketch, the continuing clarity and power of a monistic theorization of feminism emerges. Yet over time, and with the subsequent eclipse of neo-Marxism in the critical social sciences, the dialogue between feminism and Marxism has become a multi-directional conversation, between feminisms (in the plural) and a whole range of other possible angles and allies. To a far greater extent than before, feminists ask: how far can plurality and difference be embraced *within* the feminist project, and how far can feminism go in coexisting with a plurality of *other* critical perspectives?

From a monistic feminist perspective, to entertain such issues opens up a can of worms, and the resulting situation is possibly even worse than in the simpler, two-way debate with Marxism. Accordingly, MacKinnon writes: 'to proliferate "feminisms" . . . in the face of women's diversity is the latest attempt of liberal pluralism to evade the challenge women's reality poses to theory'.[3] Note how the force of MacKinnon's stance is achieved in part by the way in which pejorative connotations are attached to the very idea of pluralism. These are the same sort of connotations that I mentioned in Chapter 1, and which, ironically perhaps, also surface routinely in straight Marxist denunciations of pluralist tendencies on the Left.[4] In this register, to be pluralistic is to be liberal; it is to be evasive; it is to miss the central feature of reality; and, without that anchor in reality, it also amounts to being theoretically frivolous and self-referential.

III

According to Michele Barrett and Anne Phillips, the chief assumptions of 1970s feminist social theory are that the generalized condition of women is oppression, and that such oppression has a singular causal pattern, stemming from the very nature of the social structure.[5] Now the idea that the social structure has a partially hidden, singular, systemic logic, generating both widespread social consequences and recipes for radical change, was once held to be precisely what was exciting and liberating about critical social science. Feminists, for their part, whilst openly opposing the (male) dominant substantive traditions of structural explanation, nevertheless took over the 'structural' format for explanation, seeking their own version of 'the fundamentals of social causation'.[6] However, today, those aspirations to universality and totality, that rationalist radicalism, and those expectations of a wholly 'new subject' for theory and politics, are categorized, pejoratively, as being inherently 'modernist' and 'essentialist'. As with monism, of which they are aspects, such terms now carry grave connotative deficits, and consequently '1970s feminism' has in many respects been put on hold.

Two things in particular happened to loosen feminists' allegiance to the structural/universalist mode. First, the assertion of a singular and generalized condition of women's oppression, and the related assertion of a 'natural' or ideal interest amongst all women in its removal, had the effect of obliterating a range of vital differences amongst actual women. Paradoxically, the construction of a universal theory of women's experience and its causes rode roughshod over the right of particular groups of women to formulate and act upon their own distinctive sense of their condition, its causes and its remedies. Especially in response to the political arguments of women of colour, a 'univocal' sense of sisterhood and experience in the feminist movement gave way to an unprecedented recognition of diversity and plurality. Any feminist community of interests, and any cross-cultural assertions of unity/ uniformity were going to have to be the result of serious and tricky negotiations between autonomous, differently situated groups of women.

Second, the tidal wave of postmodernism washed up all the old notions of what a good theory of emancipatory politics should be. The very idea of 'structural' theory, for example, in which the alleged essence of the real social system is uniquely revealed by an all-powerful discourse, which then directs political practice, has been widely disavowed as being at best a convenient fiction. At worst, it is thought to be necessarily essentialist and reductive, a form of western scientific ideology, closely allied to coercive (male) styles of intellectual and political vanguardism. The problem with dominant male, bourgeois, western theories is thus felt to be as much a question of their universal, monistic and rationalist *form* as it is a matter of their political *substance*. How ironic, then, that radical substantive alternatives to male bourgeois thought, such as Marxism and feminism, have in key ways inherited precisely that spurious modern, western theoretical imagination.

Persuaded by aspects of this line of thought, many feminists have become strenuously engaged with postmodernism, to the point of describing themselves either as 'postmodernist feminists' or as 'post-feminists'. At the heart of this stance, I am arguing, is a vision of *plurality* in both the nature of social causation and in the politics of social identity. Thus, Nancy Fraser and Linda Nicholson write:

> postmodern-feminist theory would dispense with the idea of a subject of history. It would replace unitary notions of women and feminine gender identity with plural and complexly structured conceptions of social identity, treating gender as one relevant strand among others, attending also to class, race, ethnicity, age and sexual orientation.[7]

In this formulation we appear to have come full circle. Initially, it was precisely the location of gender as (at best) only one issue amongst many others that was felt to require the development of feminist theory; and it was the lack of the notion of a feminist subject of history that motivated 25 years of campaigning, con-sciousness-raising and scholarship. Now, it seems, those motivating

ideas are seriously flawed because they are insufficiently pluralist,
and it is the task of post-feminism to reassert pluralism in the name
of feminism.

IV

The question of pluralism – as mediated by debates on postmodernism – has raised difficulties and divisions within feminist theory.
Those who accept much of the postmodernist critique of western
rationalism are inclined to problematize '70s feminism' too. Thus,
to some people, earlier monistic expressions of feminism have
resulted in a very restricted frame of reference which looks
increasingly outdated. Feminist theory has become a 'prisoner of
gender' in that sense,[8] and the 'essentialist' identification of
women's oppression as a uniform condition now looks precisely
what is problematic. This is because classical feminism construed
important differences of culture, class, ethnicity, age, sexual
orientation, etc., amongst women as 'subsidiary to more basic
similarities'.[9] Whilst writers who make this point clearly have
differences amongst *women* in mind, by implying that differences
are at least as important as similarities, it is apparent that a more
general principle of 'societal pluralism' is being endorsed. In other
words, the moral and analytical weight falls on those features of any
social group's situation and culture which *distinguishes* it from those
of other groups. From that starting point, it then becomes relatively
easy to make the theoretical 'discovery' that large overarching
classifications such as social class and gender are rather cumber-
some and reductive. Also, the pluralist principle would have to be
extended to the analysis of different groups of *men* too, thus
severely limiting the power of any cross-situational generalization
about the power of men and the subordination of women.

The problem of 'societal' pluralism in recent feminist debate has
parallels at the epistemological and political levels of analysis. In
philosophical terms, few would disagree that postmodernism
appears at first to be a 'natural ally' for feminists.[10] Like postmodernists, feminists have strenuously criticized the very notions of
objectivity and universality that have underscored most dominant
paradigms in the social sciences. The whole idea of objective and
disinterested knowledge – of value-free methodology, of decisive
proof and refutation, of cognitive apprehension as set *against* the

various passions, ideologies, and interests which theories and research majestically leave trailing behind on the royal road to science – is rejected by feminists as being the ideology of the closed shop of male professional practice; and it is rejected by postmodernists as being the spurious self-glorification of the modernist theoretical imagination.

Still, in response to the dominance of modernist scientism, feminist philosophers are once again faced with a difficult choice. Those who have supported the idea of a Feminist Standpoint Epistemology (FSE) see feminism as a *replacement* for male-centred knowledge. This option is anti-pluralist, in the sense that somewhere along the line it must claim cognitive as well as political superiority for feminist knowledge and women's experience:

> In claiming that inquiry from the standpoint of women (or the feminist standpoint) can overcome the partiality and distortion of the dominant androcentric/bourgeois/Western sciences, it directly undermines the point-of-viewlessness of objectivism while refusing the relativism of interpretationism.[11]

A second option is available, though, this time a methodologically pluralist one. This second option also involves giving priority to women's experience and feminist theory, but this time the inherent 'point-of-viewness' of *all* claims to knowledge and of *all* assertions of experiential truth is openly acknowledged. FSE does not then have to go on to claim for itself a new, singular cognitive superiority, for this would once again raise the (illusory) prospect of a higher level objectivism. Rather, feminists should simply accept and contribute to the idea that there exists a heterogeneous range of (non-objectivist) methodologies and perspectives, whilst at the same time fighting their own corner where it matters.

These are difficult choices. To defend FSE in a strong sense involves taking feminist knowledge before a higher, philosophical court of appeal: the very meaning of epistemology seems inherently to require this aspiration to greater generality. However, to defend FSE as anything *less* involves either giving up altogether on the idea of an epistemological standpoint for feminism, or perhaps construing FSE as an aspect of a wider epistemic pluralism. In principle, postmodernist feminists would probably favour the outright abandonment of an epistemological standpoint for feminism, because the dethroning of epistemology is a prime aim of postmodern polemic. That way, knowledge would be suitably humbled and personalized, and customary feelings of guilt amongst those who 'lack' an official 'justificatory strategy' for their ideas could be purged. This is easier said than done, though. The suggestion that feminism should simply not be concerned with overarching theoretical-justificatory strategies is seldom actually made, and so there is plenty of ongoing grappling amongst feminists with the 'dilemmas of pluralism' in the epistemological sphere.[12]

The philosophical critique amongst feminists and postmodernists of totalizing concepts and their associated rationalism is easily translated into the specific register of political theory. The dominant 'big ideas' of Power and the State, in particular, become subject to deconstruction. In this task, many feminists are inclined to look to the work of Foucault as a resource. Thus it is sometimes argued that power should be analysed not according to a general theory of what 'it' (power) 'is', in some abstractly defined sense, nor according to what 'the state' is in some functionalist sense, nor yet in terms of the political reflection of pre-given societal/economic 'interests'. These constructions, arguably, retain a metaphysical, reified status that is no longer appropriate. Rather, a feminism suitably influenced by the work of Michel Foucault would see power both as a micro-level phenomenon and a socially pervasive one, its multiple forms and effects saturating not only official political institutions, but being 'immanent in all social relations'.[13] The resulting analytical picture not only gives full recognition to the micro-reality of power, but also to the possibility of widespread resistance and contestation. Allying Foucault to recent claims for a new style of 'radical democracy', this type of feminist theorizing is thought to encourage a less holistic (monistic) approach to research, and a more affirmative, complex sense of political practice(s).

One of the questions facing Foucauldian feminism – as in Foucault scholarship generally – is whether this theoretical approach involves a 'theory' of power at all; and if it does, whether that theory is not just a revival of pluralist politics.[14] Conscious of this latter taint, Rosemary Pringle and Sophie Watson, for example, insist that it is only 'at first sight' that poststructuralist political theory looks like a 'retreat to pluralism', and that Foucault in particular, 'though he starts with the localized and specific mechanisms and technologies of power, he is no pluralist'.[15] Two main points are offered in support of this denial of pluralism. One is that Foucault certainly *does* make connections between the particular and the general, but such interconnections 'are not to be read off from a general theory'.[16]

This argument is not convincing as it stands, because assertions of non-reductionism – the avoidance of general theory – were common in earlier political science pluralism. Conventional pluralists would have no difficulty in endorsing the (rather empiricist) proposition that the relevant forms of power have to be established through case by case analysis. Not only that, but we might question here whether a 'theory' of power is on offer at all, since the most that emerges is a pan-societal vision of micro-conflict, the nature and balance of which varies enormously. It is just this analytical 'pointillism' that has led more structurally inclined feminists to warn that 'fragmentation has gone too far', and that overly postmodernist feminism leads in effect 'towards mere empiricism'.[17]

The second argument used to differentiate poststructuralist feminist radical democratic theory from the conventional sort of pluralism is more substantial. Conventional pluralism revolves around the notion of interest groups, and the idea of pre-given interests, prior to political articulation, is not accepted in post-structuralist/postmodernist analysis. Thus, 'In post-structuralist accounts of the state, "discourse" and "subjectivity" rather than structures and interest become the key terms'.[18] Part of the point here is that interests are only constructed when groups begin to engage with the state,[19] so that politics and power need to be conceived as ongoing discursive constructions, not mere expressions of coherent, in-place societal situations.

Notwithstanding the marked differences in vocabulary, some earlier pluralists did in fact recognize that it was only in and through the specific channels of political negotiation that latent sources of political motivation in the wider society came to be recognized as interests. Moreover, the thesis of overlapping group membership in earlier versions of pluralism[20] underlines the sense that of all the potential sources of political organization and campaigning, only some crystallize into interest group activity, namely, those which realistically engage the brokering function of the state. Finally, the pluralist idea of a civic culture of democratic participation[21] is one version of how political behaviour and domination is premised on a definite 'social imaginary' – a background discourse of norms and collective self-images.

In other words, the political positions of feminist radical democracy may well differ from those of previous pluralists, but the pluralist nature of the analysis seems fairly clear all the same. The only outstanding difference is the new notion that the 'subject positions' of politics are not based on ideas of either *given* or *objective* interests.[22] But in that case, we might ask, where do subject positions come from? Perhaps we are to imagine them, as some postmodernists urge, as simply unanalysable in terms of socially emergent properties? But what, then, could it mean to see *gender* politics as entirely discursive? No answers to these questions can be found in the text I have exemplified here, partly I think because 'interests' and specific societal groups *do* in fact re-enter the scenario, and in a self-evidently pluralist sense. For example:

> A feminist orientation to the politics of difference means that we each recognize that any standpoint we take is necessarily partial and based on the way in which we are positioned in relation to class, race, educational background and a number of other factors.[23]

And:

> What intentionality [in the state] there is comes from the success with which various groupings are able to articulate their interests and hegemonize their claims.[24]

I am not at this point arguing against the type of post-feminist position under examination. Rather I am interested in the rhetoric which (unconvincingly, to me) *denies* that the kind of position on offer is pluralistic. That rhetoric seems to suggest a feeling of guilt by association, as if – even now – for feminists openly to be pluralists must be a dubious thing. If the holistic elements in feminism, along with the holism of all other isms, have been decisively deconstructed, however, feminists and poststructuralists might be expected to affirm rather than disavow their particularism and pluralism. Conventional pluralists also learned not to blanch when their focus of study was declared by radicals to be merely the 'surface' manifestations of some deeper social essence. That anti-essentialism has now spread to radicals themselves, feminists prominent amongst them.[25]

It is clear that feminists who continue to see women's politics and gender politics as stemming from a structural social situation, and who wish to pose these forms of politics as in some way privileged, must strive at some level to resist both the 'idealism' and the 'pluralism' of recent post-feminist theorizing. A 'political vision of inexhaustible heterogeneity',[26] especially a vision of inexhaustible *discursive* heterogeneity, poses serious problems for feminists because that vision takes us promptly beyond the familiar priorities of feminist theory in the modernist mode. Expressing concern about this, Christine de Stephano writes, 'with post-rationalism, '*she*' dissolves into a perplexing plurality of differences, none of which can be theoretically or politically privileged over others'.[27] Seyla Benhabib for her part straightforwardly aligns Jean-Francois Lyotard, the doyen of postmodernism, with orthodox (and ideologically liberal) pluralism in view of his projected scenario of a vast array of well-informed and technologically switched-on groups, all democratically interacting and continuously redefining themselves. Benhabib counsels fellow feminists not to fall for this prospect of a veritable 'polytheism' of language games and values,[28] because behind the enticing new terminology lies a fairly familiar and dubious pluralist picture. From a sceptical and to that extent modernist angle, Susan Bordo sums up the combined epistemic and political difficulty of post-feminist pluralism by asserting that 'reality itself may be relentlessly plural and heterogeneous, but human understanding and *interest* cannot be'.[29]

V

From philosophy to politics, then, contemporary feminist discourse expresses a series of dilemmas around issues of pluralism, issues brought to the fore by postmodernist themes. Postmodernism, indeed, can be redescribed perhaps as the generalized affirmation of pluralism and heterogeneity. Put that way, of course, many feminists are understandably tempted to defend aspects of monism and modernism, because it must be doubtful whether feminism 'can survive as a radical politics if it gives up on a hierarchy of theory'.[30] Yet this is just what relentless pluralism dictates.

Given the dialectical nature of all argument and rhetoric, there often emerges in due course the prospect of a third way, a synthesis, between two apparently locked and contrary options in social theory. So too in feminism, where probably the majority of thinkers are neither so wedded to postmodernism as to disavow the label of feminism altogether, nor so committed to modernism as to deny the insights of postmodern pluralism, and certainly not the contemporary resonance of the politics of difference. Thus Anne Phillips maintains that whilst the politics of difference is a necessary blow against dogmatic universalism in political theory, none the less 'feminism cannot afford to situate itself *for* difference and *against* universality'.[31] Similarly, Barrett and Phillips argue that 'difference is not an absolute' and that the very polarization of equality/difference such that these terms are perceived to be contrary to one another, might usefully be deconstructed.[32]

This line of thinking follows an important tendency amongst 'moderate' postmodernists to try to avoid the pitfalls of supposedly 'extreme' or 'strong' postmodernism by reconceptualizing the nature of the postmodernist intervention. For example, it is often thought that postmodernism supports an 'anything goes' relativism as a counterblow to modernist objectivism. However, it could be that the whole point of postmodernism is simply to unlock or deconstruct this very restrictive opposition itself. This gambit can be repeated for any number of familiar conceptual oppositions: materialism versus idealism, holism versus particularism, science versus ideology, structure versus agency, general versus particular, and so on. If postmodernism is seen as the imaginative deconstruction of such polarities rather than seen as simply constituting the 'flip side' of the various modernist orthodoxies, then all-or-nothing choices between modernist and postmodernist modes within particular discourses such as feminism might begin to lose their intractable quality.

In that spirit, moderate postmodernists are less concerned to counter the rationalism and the ordering impulse of modernist modes of thinking with new brands of irrationalism and intellectual disorder; rather the point would be to urge the acceptance of ambivalence, hybridity and hesitation as legitimate aspects of intellectual and political endeavour today. Feminism's own place at the forefront of postmodern debates is actually reinforced by this modified notion of postmodernism as ambivalence[33] since few feminist writers fall unambiguously into the categories of 'straight' modernist on the one hand or 'wild' postmodernist on the other. Thus Jane Flax, for example, who more than many feminist writers embraces postmodernist styles of reasoning, continues to worry about the loss of the idea of subjective integrity in the fashionable notion that not only groups but each individual *self* or subjectivity is a radically plural and fragmented phenomenon. She also conducts a familiar radical-structural critique of the conventional pluralism that she admits forms an element of poststructuralist political theory.[34] At the same time, whilst I have cited a number of writers who strongly resist the postmodernization of feminism, not one amongst them has failed to acknowledge the insights and value of postmodernist considerations – at least when posed as questions rather than as solutions.

Pluralism conceived not as the positive affirmation of multiplicity and heterogeneity for its own sake, but rather conceived as openness to persuasion within a principled range of alternatives, is not something, I would imagine, that would cause serious disagreement amongst feminists. In that spirit, Sandra Harding argues that it represents a strength, not a weakness, for feminists to feel 'caught' about the aims and nature of a justificatory strategy for feminism today.[35] Admittedly, no formally coherent resolution has as yet emerged from this 'positive' ambivalent stance. But in so far as the attempt to hold on to something in both modernist and postmodernist versions of feminism reflects the different, sometimes conflicting, legitimate theoretical and political needs of women today, the tension between those versions is arguably not only unavoidable but desirable. The implication here is that it is only when we are under the sway of a coercive modernist code of pure logic that we are inclined to feel bad about our lack of complete coherence and rigour. Perhaps the ultimate contribution of postmodernism is simply to loosen up that sense of intellectual 'completion' and the rigid mental–moral set that goes along with it.

That trail of 'quasi-' or 'ambivalent' postmodern reflection is undoubtedly attractive. It captures the spirit of feminist debates as exemplified in the two keynote collections of essays I have chosen to concentrate upon for the purposes of this discussion. It also highlights the pervasive, rather tiresome presence in all social theorizing of persistent dualisms, and puts forward an interesting way of approaching them. At the same time, I believe we need to be conscious of the 'constructed' and 'weighted' nature of this favoured 'middle way' position. For one thing, the discourse of 'ambivalence' tends to be framed as, precisely, a moderate *postmodern* move. Definitively, however, ambivalence cuts *both* ways, and so it is perhaps inappropriate that the ordering, structuring, modernist half of the equation tends (as it does) to take a back seat in the drive for a new formula.

Second, ambivalence seems to indicate a condition of being in a quandary, of feeling torn between two equally persuasive viewpoints. However, to see our intellectual condition in this way might again, and paradoxically, be somewhat reductive of the complexity of our weighted preferences. We seldom feel torn exactly equally between a pair or range of options each of which we can see might be appealing in some way. Third, it might just be that the construction of theoretical dualisms of one sort or another is simply unavoidable – and useful, even – in developing the elements of any intelligible and distinctive framework of thought. Indeed, what would we do without them? So whilst we may well come to think of persistent dualisms as overly rigid, or as in due course in dire need of dissolution, or as requiring creative synthesizing, they do nevertheless have an age-old habit of reasserting themselves, even in the fabric of supposedly new, synthetic projects.

Fourth, the moral points tend to go to postmodernism when talk of overcoming persistent and unhelpful dualisms is in the air. Yet we need to recall that 'modernism', complete with its governing problematic and polar opposites, is itself the discursive *product* of postmodernism. Modernism in that sense was invented by postmodernism as a self-defining strategy. As such, the various summary portraits of modernism, the Enlightenment Project, foundationalism, logocentrism, and so on, that circulate on the 'most wanted' posters in postmodernist texts need to be regarded as tremendous imaginative truncations of a more complex and variegated intellectual history. In any case, with moderate postmodernism, when couched in dilemmatic form as open-endedness or ambivalence, it is often the *continuities* between postmodernism and modernism which stand out, not their intrinsic antagonisms. Such considerations, I think, indicate that however ostensibly appealing it may be, a 'third way' between postmodernist, ultra-pluralist feminism on the one hand, and modernist, monistic feminism on the other has not been easy to forge. In that respect, the debate around pluralism within feminist work encapsulates precisely the wider intellectual situation.

Tracking
Pluralism: 1

I

Having introduced some pluralist ideas, and indicated how 'plural-ism' continues to act as a short fuse in theoretical and political debates, it is time to explore further its intellectual history and disciplinary reach. In its most basic meaning, pluralism signals a theorized preference for multiplicity over unicity, and for diversity over uniformity. The conceptual logic of pluralism thus pits it dialectically against 'monism', whatever field of human investi-gation we care to consider. Virtually every specialist discourse could thus be expected to exhibit, periodically, some aspect of the pluralism/monism interface, even if pluralism is not the 'official name' for a recognized school of thought within that field. In that sense, any intellectual effort whatsoever to drag diversity and multiplicity out of the clutches of apparently monistic alternatives could be said to constitute a pluralist theoretical move. The possibilities for recruitment into the broad church of pluralism then of course become almost infinite, with relevant domains including not only the human sciences but the natural sciences too. The Copernican revolution in astronomy, the splitting of the atom, relativity theory, quantum physics, chaos theories, non-big bang cosmologies – these and countless other paradigmatic develop-ments in the 'harder' sciences could be portrayed as pluralist moves in a generic sense, since they render distinctly 'centric' and limited the prevailing doctrines which they supersede, and since they multiply the resident basic entities of the discourse. Moreover, such breakthroughs – sometimes very explicitly – encourage a sense of methodological and epistemological pluralism, the idea that for substantive progress in knowledge to occur, a number of quite different metatheoretical horizons must actively be embraced.

Thankfully, it is impossible to track the emergence of pluralist currents according to this extremely broad sense; the more manageable strategy for the next two chapters is to portray only some of the important themes and theories which have been consciously dubbed as pluralist. Also, I focus upon strands of thought in which the pluralism in question has had a distinctly political or moral ring to it, even if – as in the philosophical variants – the ring is heard only in the distance. Though related in ways I will touch upon, the labelled versions of pluralism that I feature cover a surprising range of enquiry. Appropriately enough, down the years there have been a number of positions claiming to be pluralist, and each of these pluralisms has had its own specific impulse and focus. My approach is to try to capture something of the particularity of each pluralist episode, whilst at the same time emphasizing that 'pluralism' in all contexts remains quite an abstract and generic term, its root meaning indicating an opposition to monism, and the recognition/ celebration of multiplicity. The very adoption of the signature label, therefore, does, I think, create a common subtext across discourses that otherwise might have little in common.

II

Within philosophical discourse, issues of monism versus pluralism go back to the ancient Greeks. Parmenides posited the essential, indivisible and eternal Oneness of being, whilst Empedocles and later 'atomists' such as Democritus by contrast held that the various elements and kinds in the world had substantial identities all of their own. These early pluralist philosophers also projected a fresh sense of the dynamism and necessity of contingent *change*, as against the typically *static* feel of monism. This battle of 'the One and the Many' has been rerun many times since the ancients, and it tends to get reinvented with every new epoch and generation.

Interestingly, even today, the entry for pluralism in philosophical dictionaries usually invites us to look up 'monism' as the relevant guiding antonym, suggesting that it is monistic theories of substance, spirit and knowledge that have 'led the way' in humanity's intellectual quest, and that pluralist currents are essentially reactive to, and 'deconstructive' of, monism. Whilst this lexical ordering may be appropriate in the longer view of things, in some ways it feels skewed, given that the break-up and disenchantment of unitary notions of the One, the World, Mind, Matter, Reality, and History have been in determined progress at least since the early twentieth century. The scientific revolutions of the early modern period had already created the conditions for the assertion of a positive pluralist ontology framed against a background orthodoxy of misty monism. In what was perhaps the most dazzling re-enactment of the 'Greek' issue, Leibniz in the seventeenth century constructed a highly original philosophical pluralism in response to Spinoza's pantheistic vision of an infinite, logically necessary Substance, wherein God and nature are one. Leibniz's 'mona-dology' – the assertion of an infinite series of particulars, related only 'externally' to one another – strikes a definite modern note, in that the identity of each monad is given by its logically unique position and 'point of view' within the plenum of monads.

With the construction of such a radical pluralist metaphysic, however, Leibniz also confronted the theoretical and moral diffi-culty which has attended that kind of vision ever since: can we humans, finite beings that we are, actually *live* with the apparent lack of structure and purpose which rigorous perspectivalism and endless individualization seem to entail? Unable for his part to countenance straight physicalism and contingency, Leibniz himself famously contrived his monads as *souls* rather than simply as 'points'. The monads could then be finally reconnected in the greater order of things under the good auspices of the principle of sufficient reason and the will of God, the ultimate Creator and Orchestrator of the monadic hierarchies.

The ascent and fall of Hegelianism in European intellectual culture represents an episode having a more emphatic pluralist resolution than anything that went before. Encompassing key debates in the fields of philosophy, political theory, legal doctrine and ecclesiastical thought, pluralism emerged as a concerted and confident critical project attuned to the ethos and dynamism of the new twentieth century. As with most epochal encounters in which cultural hegemony is the prize, what is impressive about Anglo-American pluralism at this time is the ease with which links are made between different levels of abstraction and across different knowledge specialisms. Of course, in spite of its speculative and abstract philosophical form, Hegelianism was always very self-consciously just this sort of totalizing world-view, its monistic impulse ensuring from the outset a very intimate tie-up between the metaphysical fabric and its 'application' in terms of secular history in the nation state. So if pluralism was going to be effective, if it was going to set the terms of the new intellectual agenda, it needed to take on something of that breadth of the dominant Hegelian paradigm.

III

A typical strategy of philosophical intervention in the context of cultural challenge is to embrace the new by constructing previous orthodoxies as dogmatic, rationally indefensible, and even faintly ridiculous. In the same way, the radical, progressive novelty of the successor viewpoint is pointed up, exaggerated, and affected. For those who wish to uphold or develop the already existing framework, a common tactic is to warn sternly against extreme versions of the new iconoclastic outlook, though in practice some milder version of it can usually be accepted and 'managed' without too much difficulty. In the case of the pluralist challenge to monism, I want to present three philosophical performances of 1907–8 as a module of this rhetorical dialectic.

In 1907, Bertrand Russell, having recently experienced his 'revolt into pluralism', polemicized against 'the monistic theory of truth' at the Aristotelian Society in London.[1] The postive aspect of Russell's stance became known as 'logical atomism', and the negative or critical part of it went like this:

> the logic that I should wish to combat maintains that in order thoroughly to know any one thing, you must know all its relations and all its qualities, all the propositions in fact in which that thing is mentioned; and you deduce of course from that that the world is an interdependent whole ... of course it is clear that since everything has relations to everything else, you cannot know all the facts of which a thing is a constituent without having some knowledge of everything in the universe.[2]

Just a few months later, in his Oxford lecture series of 1908, published as *A Pluralistic Universe*, William James for his part argued that

> It is curious how little countenance radical pluralism has ever had from philosophers. Whether materialistically or spiritualistically

minded, philosophers have always aimed at cleaning up the litter
with which the world is apparently filled . . . As compared with all
these rationalising pictures, the pluralistic empiricism which I profess offers but a sorry appearance. It is a turbid, muddled, gothic
sort of affair, without a sweeping outline and with little pictorial no-
bility.[3]

In such arguments, often ironical, Hegelian monism – the existing
orthodoxy – is made to seem quite absurd and alien, 'a metaphysical monster' (James) which defies 'common sense' (Russell). On
that basis, the successor pluralist position is legitimated through
the startlingly 'obvious' suggestion that, very simply, there exist
many separate things in the world. As a strategy of demolition, this
pluralist critique undoubtedly made a major impact, reversing the
philosophical priorities of the previous epoch. It entitled James to
pronounce triumphantly: 'The prestige of the absolute has rather
crumbled in our hands'.[4]

For all its critical effect in the downfall of Hegelianism, pluralism nevertheless lacked coherence as a positive outlook, perhaps
explaining why to this day pluralism gets defined, philosophically,
as in the main an *oppositional* programme. To remain only with
our cited authors, neither Russell nor James in truth possessed the
'common-sense' outlook that played such an important rhetorical
role in their texts and conversations. Nor did the main lines of
thought of these authors ultimately coincide. Russell's residual scientism led him strenuously to oppose James's pragmatism,[5] while
James's warnings of the dangers of 'vicious intellectualism' in stri-
ving to characterize the ultimate constituents of the world seemed
to him applicable not only to Hegelian idealism but also very much
to static 'particularist' alternatives, such as Russell's own theory of
logical atomism.[6]

Drawing on Henri Bergson's notion of creative evolution, James
was keen to argue that, in experience, we witness and work with
things *in the making*, not with fixed, abstract ontologies. James's
brand of pluralism, then, was not intended to be just another 'con-
ceptualist' version of what sorts of things must necessarily exist in
the world; rather it expressed an openness to the partial, 'process-
ual' truths of both 'the one' and 'the many'.[7] Triggering an impulse
for pragmatic accommodation that came to characterize American
political science for many decades after, James probably wanted to
avoid taking sides between exaggerated polar extremes in matters

ontological, declaring instead that 'compromise and mediation are inseparable from the pluralistic philosophy'.[8]

With that significant amendment to pluralist metatheory, James (like Leibniz before him) then confronted the apparent *purposelessness* which absolute contingency threatens to visit upon pluralists. Urging us to break out of the 'cold' world of donnish rational abstraction, James saw philosophies as providing important expressions of 'intimacy' between humanity and the universe more generally.[9] Pluralism is particularly appropriate in this context, he thought, since the very incompleteness of its world picture, its disconnections and hesitations, does force us to seek to regain wholeness, but by way of *practice*, and indeed by way of faith, rather than through further exercises in ratiocination.

In a third public lecture series begun in 1907, the Cambridge philosopher James Ward sought strategically to incorporate something like James's pluralism into a broader idealist picture. In other words, Ward tried to blunt the novelty of the emerging pluralist paradigm by blending some of its elements back into a version of the dominant perspective. He achieved this by critically exposing some underlying dilemmas and ironies that he felt were generated by the pluralist turn. In particular, Ward drew attention to what he called the problem of the 'upper limit' of pluralism.[10] If pluralism is strictly adhered to, he argued, it begins to reveal a rigorous 'absolutism' of its own, in that plurality and differentiation can run on almost to infinity. This is one apparent internal inconsistency in the doctrine. Not only that, however: in order to be intellectually reconciled to, and to feel spiritually at home in, a discontinuous panoply of particulars, *some kind of unifying move* in the pluralist picture is often signalled; some higher principle, either of reason or of faith, which makes overall sense of ontological dispersion. Now idealism still has advantages over pluralism here, Ward maintained, and can even incorporate the latter to an extent, because idealism is precisely the attempt explicitly to articulate together the dual modes of reason and spirit, unity and difference. The implication here is that as soon as philosophical pluralists embark on a serious justificatory strategy – and how could they not? – they become *de facto* idealists, in the sense of needing to rescue some sort of subjective harmony out of actual discord, unity out of difference.

The contributions of Russell, James and Ward, I think, reveal something of that important early twentieth-century moment in pluralist philosophy, and they also uncannily foreshadow the conceptual discussions of pluralism taking place in our own time. They also provoke questions about how the abstract discourse of philosophy connects with more concrete concerns. In fact, just as our three emblematic philosophers were taking their bow, the Owl of Minerva was preparing to take flight. Pluralism was already migrating to a new domain – in political theory.

IV

In a paper given at Columbia University in 1915, Harold Laski set the terms for a decisive translation of pluralism from a philosophic to an institutional register by asserting that 'What the Absolute is to metaphysics, that is the State to political theory'.[11] In order to facilitate a favourable reception for European political pluralism in the United States, Laski also latched on to a single sentence in James's *Pluralistic Universe* in which the pragmatist philosopher likened his pluralistic ontology to a federal republic (as opposed to an empire or kingdom).[12] Laski's intention was not only to draw parallels between philosophy and politics however. He also wanted to wrest the ideas of pluralism and the state out of their philosophical cocoon altogether. In the hands of the Hegelians, Laski argued, the state was treated as an ideal, a Platonic form. Yet this abstract 'superstructure' of metaphysical reflection, he insisted, stemmed from a very concrete institutional basis:

> The state is today the one compulsory form of association . . . the area of its enterprise has consistently grown until today there is no field of human activity over which, in some degree, its pervading influence may not be detected.[13]

The pluralist battle against Hegelian statism was couched in part as a battle against philosophy itself because, paradoxically, Hegelianism, for all its misty abstraction, was in a sense more political and more progressive than some earlier philosophical currents. The chief alternative, ontological pluralism, had been traditionally cast as a severely atomistic doctrine, and the most obvious ideological translation of this picture is some kind of liberal *individualism*. In that context, the Hegelian emphasis on unity in difference, and on the common good, was attractive. In that way it played a significant part in the ascendancy of the 'New Liberalism' of the late nineteenth century in England,[14] which offered a collectivist (but non-socialist) ideological alternative to the social and ethical ravages of *laissez-faire* capitalism.

Political pluralists of Laski's stamp were certainly opposed to state collectivism, but not at all in the name of societal individualism. Rather, these pluralists wanted to promote a version of collectivism *below* the level of the nation state, chiefly by recognizing corporations and associations as independent formations and interests.

Just as they knew the attractions of ontological pluralism, so the Hegelians were sharp enough to recognize the appeal of political pluralism. For example, the leading idealist Bernard Bosanquet tried to forestall the challenge of 'legal pluralists' such as F.W.Maitland and Otto von Gierke by asserting that pluralism and absolutism were, properly understood, 'fully in accord'. Such plural collectivities as corporations, Bosanquet insisted, actually depended for their effective coordination on the legitimacy of the idea of a higher level common will. Without a strong emphasis on coordination and harmony, pluralism would descend into institutional chaos.[15] Rather than attempting to refute this kind of rejoinder in its own terms, it seemed to pluralists like Laski more pertinent to point to the damage that 'absolute' philosophizing was doing in real political life. This was already a strong inclination before 1914, but pluralist concerns about the adventures of the Absolute were considerably deepened by the perceived growth of the 'moloch' state during the Great War.

The political pluralists thus wanted to 'discredit'[16] the idea of the state by challenging its philosophical basis, by rejecting its social legitimacy, and by offering an alternative account of political sovereignty. This alternative project has been well described in the following way:

> Its key features were an awareness of groups and associations as the depositories of loyalties and obligations; of the principle of function as the central differentiating criterion in society; of the state as one functional association amongst others; and of the need to create an organizational structure which recognized the rights of associations to substantial self-government whilst harmonizing the relation between the associations themselves to meet the requirements of the community as a whole.[17]

Pluralism at this time, it should be noted, was as much a critique of the emerging orthodoxy of representative democracy as it was a critique of statism. The legal pluralists argued that corporate bodies which were endowed with a merely 'fictional' legal status – companies, trusts, churches, unions, and so on – should be treated as perfectly substantial and 'real'. Political pluralists of the Left such as Laski and G.D.H. Cole wanted to go further and show that it was actually the twin ruling idea of the state-*and*-the-individual that was most problematical. A franchise based on individual rights and territorial representation within the sovereign state, pluralists argued, inadequately reflects our *collective* social existence, and sets up a structure whereby an all-powerful state stands over against a mass of isolated individuals. A system of *functional* representation, on the other hand, assumes politics to be a matter of debate and decision-making amongst social *groups* – most notably those which perform key economic roles. The Left pluralist argument went on to claim that if recognized associational forms were to operate as self-governing *democracies*, then a high degree of political participation in the society would be guaranteed, together with a better informed and well-motivated political culture.

Pluralist political theory in this vein tended to be socialistic, with a particular emphasis (in Cole especially) on the democratic socialist role of the 'guilds' of producers.[18] The pluralist literature did allow for considerable diversity in the functional principles according to which associational bodies participated in the commonwealth, however. The concerns of the influential political and ecclesiastical writer J.N. Figgis, for example, illustrate this feature. Figgis sought first to establish the proper basis for authority within the church, and second to theorize the role of the churches within a democratic and mainly secular society.[19] In both cases Figgis strongly supported a diversity of values, and insisted upon the vital political potential embodied in the *voluntary* constitution of associations. Accordingly, the specific loyalties and principles upon which voluntary associations were founded should be officially recognized and respected by the nation state, Figgis argued. Such public recognition of plurality would greatly enhance both the will and the ability of associations to do public service. The state (and also the church itself) was thus best viewed not as a uniform and primary body in itself, but rather as a 'society of societies', with people's allegiance to the state being conditional upon their more immediate allegiances (i.e. to the associations) being accepted and valued as the primary source of action and identification.

After a long period of neglect, the tradition of English political pluralism that I have just discussed has been rediscovered. It had a substantial pedigree in philosophical and political analysis. It had no difficulty in moving from the abstract realm of theory to that of institutional reform. And its identification of the serious democratic deficits of the liberal nation state form – disproportional representation, individualist calculation, territorial constituencies, minority governments, 'elective despotism', and so on – was both powerful and prescient. Moreover, its *associationalist* conception of the good political society remains a potent source of democratic reappraisal today.[20]

V

If English pluralism was premised on a critical approach to both metaphysics and statism, the discourse nevertheless stayed focused on the question of the *state*, and on the urgency of an assessment of the political consequences of our abstract philosophical predilections. With the migration of pluralism not only from philosophy to politics, but from Europe to the United States, these normative and analytical dimensions began to drop out of sight. William James had coined another term for his outlook of ontological pluralism, namely 'radical empiricism', and it was under this banner that American pluralism established its self-image as the empirical social science of political behaviour. From A.F. Bentley's 1908 text *The Process of Government* through to the more sophisticated writings of Robert Dahl and Charles E. Lindblom spanning the last four decades, pluralism became essentially the study of the formation and intermediation of political interest groups as a precondition of competitive liberal democracy.

Within this political science tradition, there has always been a normative tension, in which a 'conventional' pluralist perspective is countered by a noticeably more 'critical' outlook.[21] The 'conventional' pluralist scenario had five main planks. The first was conformity to the prevailing sociological conception that industrial society evolves in an ever more complex way through functional differentiation and technological progress. The citizenry of such a social formation might thus be expected to be increasingly interdependent and well-informed. Second, we have the belief that social groups are the basic units of interaction and socialization. The importance of groups is not to be interpreted in a collectivist way, however. Rather, due to advanced social differentiation, groups are constituted as being relatively small-scale and as having *overlapping memberships*; individuals are formed within a variety of group contexts, and these group contexts are not to be regarded in terms of large scale functional classes, after the Marxist (and the English socialist-pluralist) manner. Group interests, then, are not pre-given; they emerge in the process of specific group formation, and indeed 'interests' often only get fully defined and expressed when governmental handling of citizen concerns is revealed as overly-selective. In this vein, the American pluralists sometimes wrote of political groups having a 'potential' rather than actual existence and impact.

Third, in conventional pluralism the state is interpreted as a 'governmental process', a project of inclusion aimed at striking a responsive balance between competing interests and demands. The metaphors for this aspect of conventional pluralist theory vary intriguingly; variously the state has been conceived as a weathervane, a switchboard, a broker, an arbitrator, and a general manager. The whole political process has been cast by turns as a social physics of pressures and counter-pressures, as an equilibrium curve, as the demand for and supply of political goods, and as an evolutionary sequence of competition and organic adaptation.

Fourth, the pluralist literature is closely allied to research on the modern civic culture of the democracies. In *The Civic Culture*, for example, Almond and Verba conducted a comparative survey of democratic values aimed at isolating the conditions of democratic stability.[22] In the array of criteria used, citizens' multiple membership of civic organizations, and their elementary informedness of political events were particularly highlighted. Overall, the conclusion was that a basic citizen allegiance to, and participation in, the democratic civic culture existed, and that we should not be too surprised or disappointed that it is not higher. This is because of the importance of civic *trust* in a democracy; overactivity in the demos might actually be a sign that the pluralist system is *not*, in fact, working properly, that interest groups are *not* prepared to compromise in the overarching interest of social harmony and material progress for all. Successful liberal democracy thus demands of its people only a *limited* political knowledge and an *implicit* commitment to the system. Civic trust in leaders, and leaders' responsiveness to (potential) interest group claims might be expected to do the rest.

The fifth dimension of conventional pluralism has already been touched upon. Its methodology was intended to be empiricist and descriptive: grand theorizing around abstract quasi-philosophical themes was regarded as being out of touch with the modern world. Ideologizing in political thought had to give way to input–output research on political decision-making, and to a modestly affirmative attitude to 'our' admittedly imperfect, but at least stable and prosperous, western democracies.

The *critical* variant of political science pluralism only came fully into view when some of the key pluralists themselves entered a new, distinctly 'revisionist' phase through the 1970s and into the 1980s; but the elements of the alternative had been circulating through the 1960s, using resources drawn from Marxist thought and from 'conflict theory'.[23] The most persistent theme of critical pluralism was not so much that conventional pluralism's values were mistaken, but that these values most definitely did not map on to the western nations in the way that 'complacent' pluralists seemed to think. Eclipsed and threatened by the hegemonic Americanism of the 1950s, critical pluralism re-emerged under the combined impact of social strife in the American cities during the 1960s, the Vietnam war, and the Watergate scandal.

One chief revisionist contention was that social groups (e.g. families, peer groups, income and workplace classes) tend to be far more 'fixed' and more influential for individual behaviour – and much less benign in their influence – than was supposed in the conventional view. Group interests and social characteristics, in other words, are consolidated *prior* to, and not merely 'constructed' in, the political process. Additionally, the pluralist belief in the relatively 'neutral' response of the governmental process to societal pressures was also found to be highly questionable. Indeed, 'government' in the sense of *the apparatus of the state* was hardly theorized at all in the conventional texts. Yet states and governments arguably form the most important interest groups of all, and their power is consolidated through their extraordinary control of material resources and surveillance capacities.

Moreover, given the economic stakes involved in the reproduction of the American 'industrial-military complex', the state policy agenda is inevitably constructed with a view to its impact on the key business sectors, and on those parts of the state which are not noticeably subject to democratic accountability. Conventional pluralism, at best, under-emphasized those deep structural constraints on the democratic process. In relation to the idea of a democratic civic culture, the literature of citizen 'trust' came to look more like an apology for apathy than a celebration of citizen competence, since it rested content with very low indexes of democratic involvement in the interests of order and stability. As for the ethos of spreading information and trust throughout the social body, this was increasingly seen – by pluralists themselves – as simply a matter of indoctrination in the norms of the status quo.

In these criticisms of conventional pluralism, close attention is paid to the implicit assumptions that are made about the beneficence of limited democracy, and much has also been made about the lack of pluralist attention to the ways in which 'non-decisions' in the political agenda continually serve to reproduce the socioeconomic order. Such criticisms stretch beyond the empirical 'findings' of political science and strike at the very heart of its theoretical and methodological tenets too. Put simply, behaviourist and empiricist canons of investigation are incapable of detecting or theorizing the 'structural' constraints which frame any particular balance of power. Under the banner of scientific rectitude, the dominant paradigm, it was argued, effectively implied a conservative value-stance. Focusing on *overt* behaviour and ostensible political claims and concessions, the *underlying* social realities were being ignored. The critical alternative, in theorizing politics, thus required a firm rejection of 'descriptivism' and in effect was endorsing a revival of the genre of sociohistorical theorizing on a large scale. It also involved a broad-based assault on the illusion that political theory and political scientists are above or beyond 'ideology'.

The general influence of Marxism and other radical perspectives on these critical pluralist reflections should be evident. But however unconventional the critical pluralists became, they have still resisted the strong structuralist and 'classist' propositions of historical materialism. Accordingly, various efforts to manage a synthesis between elements of Marxism and critical pluralism have been attempted over the years. Such mergers have been undertaken, it should be noted, as much for 'scientific' reasons as ideological ones. For example, one of the most prominent efforts to mould elements taken from Marxism and pluralism into a new political science paradigm has been the research programme known as 'neo-corporatism'. Winning considerable support from the mid-1970s to the mid-1980s, the neo-corporatist perspective reintroduced the notion that *the state itself* must be seen as forming a crucial strategic bargaining interest, and indeed that there is an ongoing bargaining process within the state, as well as between certain state agencies and those 'peak associations' which represent the main socio-economic interests in the wider society. In this way, the conventional pluralist scenario of a broad array of voluntary pressure groups, operating as if in a political 'free market', was unambiguously ditched. At the same time, neo-corporatism, whilst 'structurally' orientated in that sense, was not at all committed in advance to characterizing the modern state as always operating essentially as a *capitalist* state. Indeed, the balance and direction of corporatist intermediation was not to be pre-empted by reference to any very specific theoretical grid. For a time, then, neo-corporatism looked to be the sprightly new replacement for those tired old warhorses Marxism and pluralism.[24]

In spite of its early promise, however, neo-corporatism faded rather badly during the revival of neo-liberalism and the 'rolling back of the state' in the advanced capitalist nations during the 1980s. Moreover, some measure of agreement has developed amongst proponents and opponents alike that, in the end, the nature of state interests was theorized little better in neo-corporatism than it had been in orthodox pluralism. This is because the neo-corporatist scenario was not in fact as dramatically anti-pluralist as was sometimes claimed. In particular, the neo-corporatists manifestly retained the background conception of a political bargaining process in which the various competing interests are approximately equal in strength and status – a central pluralist assumption. Moreover, when neo-corporatism came up for revision, it moved even further towards pluralism; there was a creeping feeling that in focusing on the peak associations of industry and the economy, and in highlighting the notion of functional representation, neo-corporatism had betrayed a distinct 'productionist' bias. Latterly, this emphasis has been corrected through neo-corporatists emphasizing more explicitly the significance of *consumption* groupings, of ethical and lifestyle movements, and the 'cultural politics' of group representation. In this vein, one leading writer has claimed that with these 'culturalist' additions, neo-corporatism has been separated even further from conventional pluralism.[25] This claim is very doubtful, however; the enhanced role of sociocultural characteristics in the neo-corporatist picture actually draws it closer to pluralism. In fact, the independent theoretical basis of neo-corporatism was never really theorized satisfactorily. From the start, as well as including the pluralistic conception of politics as group bargaining, the neo-corporatist literature readily encompassed writers whose approach to the process of state-sponsored interest intermediation was fairly straightforwardly Marxist.[26]

A rather unexpected result comes out of these considerations. Critical pluralism developed in the slipstream of the revival of Marxism in the 1970s, and through the 'continentalization' of American political thought more generally. Neo-corporatism, for its part, got off the ground as a theory and research programme explicitly framed as superseding both Marxism and pluralism. Yet it is Marxism, the sworn enemy of conventional pluralism, and neo-corporatism, the all-modern synthesis, that have most obviously come to grief in recent years. In the case of Marxism, of course, this is partly a matter of its perceived political obsolescence, but also – long prior to the fall of communism from 1989 on – persistent, demoralizing doubts have been growing amongst radical theorists about the rigidity of Marxism's anti-pluralist theoretical idiom. In the case of neo-corporatism, its dependence upon the framework of the nation state, its emphasis on economic and state-centred bargaining, and its recent expression of compensatory 'culturalism' have all served to undermine its promise as a new middle way. Perhaps the chief merit of neo-corporatism was not that it provided a new theoretical model at all, but rather that it succeeded in impressing upon theorists and researchers of many shades the vital importance of the 'meso-level' of social enquiry, forcing all relevant theories to focus their attention on concrete institutional arrangements and organized collective actors.[27] Be that as it may, with Marxism and neo-corporatism shoved out into the wings, we are now confronted with the rather surprising scenario in which sociopolitical pluralism, somewhat dazed, rusty and hesitant, has been summoned to rise up and take the theoretical centre-stage once again.

4
Tracking Pluralism: 2

I

Any revived pluralist perspective on the advanced democracies today faces two crucial issues that were not so prominent in the heyday of conventional pluralism. The first concerns the extent to which pluralism 'applies' to sociopolitical configurations *outside* the liberal metropolis. Relatedly, there is the issue of how far the pluralist metropolis itself is being changed by global migrancy, bringing 'non-western' people and cultures more visibly into the forefront of political and intellectual consideration. In fact, a strong post-war tradition of analysis and advocacy was developed precisely to address that first question, going under the rubric of 'the plural society' model. In portaying this genre of pluralism, I will also suggest that it has significance for the second question too. One important aspect of the plural society strand has been its embrace of the idea of 'legal pluralism', but since these two labels are not exactly co-terminous, I discuss the latter separately. The third pluralist 'moment' I deal with in this chapter, 'interpretative pluralism', is rather different from the other two, being more obviously methodological in focus. The question of method in literary and cultural theory today is above all centred around the business of embracing 'otherness'. Thus, notions of the western 'canon' and 'right' interpretations in academic disciplines are under intense scrutiny precisely because they have not adequately re-flected wider developments in the plural society at large. These disciplines are therefore seen as a site of struggle, in which a full and pluralistic cultural inclusiveness is at stake.

II

In many ways, the nature of the plural society analysis is, confusingly, just the opposite to that of conventional political pluralism. Where the latter was concerned with the advanced industrial democracies, the plural society notion was specifically addressed to late colonial political formulas in tropical societies, particularly southeast Asia. Pluralism in the West signified the modern citizen's membership of overlapping groups, equal access to political goods, and a general consensus over values. By marked contrast, the plural society theorists described the consolidation of a number of pre-modern ethnic identities within those contrived nation states that had been restructured by colonialist population movements. 'Pluralism' was the term used to describe this very non-consensual situation of *institutionalized* differences and inequalities amongst clearly distinguished cultural segments. The modernizing strategy of the dominant groups in these plural (= 'underdeveloped') societies was to encourage speedy integration in the economic marketplace, but also (in the interim at least) it was accepted that a significant degree of separatism in the social and political spheres was desirable. So whereas pluralism within the civil society of the advanced democracies seemed to be a matter of sociocultural heterogeneity and mobility, these features were almost completely absent in the societies originally analysed in the plural society model.

For the most elaborate theorist of the plural society, M.G. Smith,[1] the existence of *variety* in cultural values and practices does not in itself warrant the title of pluralism at all, since the all-important factor of publicly consolidated marks of social difference may not result from cultural variety *per se*. Rather, it is only when cultural difference is thoroughly embedded in a system of institutionalized social practices, practices which set apart one group from another in the framing of the polity, that pluralism 'proper' can be said to exist. Furthermore, for writers like Smith, societal pluralism may well be regarded as having a 'structural' nature; that would be in cases where the material resources of the society in question, and its legal statuses, are distributed in an unambiguously hierarchical and even coercive way. Slavery would probably be the paradigm of 'structural pluralism' in that sense, further reinforcing the paradox that the two traditions of political analysis which have most explicitly claimed the 'pluralism' label would seem to embody sharply divergent analytical and political priorities.

Following the lead of J.S. Furnivall,[2] who appears to have coined the term 'plural society', Smith in particular takes the analysis in a different direction from the conventional pluralist theorists of democracy. Not only does Smith's brand of conceptualization offer a more explicit conceptualization of pluralism than occurs in most conventional political science discussions of pluralism, it seems much closer to Marxism in impetus, especially the Marxist genre of 'underdevelopment' analysis. However, this appearance is rather deceptive. For one thing, Smith's theory of pluralism is more *taxonomical* than *explanatory*. By this I mean that his categories of analysis are comprehensive and informative, but only as an elaborate mapping exercise, covering neatly the different sub-species of plural society according to the degree to which cultural difference is embedded in institutional rules and practices. What even the best of these authors do *not* give us, in other words, is a causal and functional account of the origins and dynamics of the plural societies in question.

Like conventional pluralism in this respect, the terminology of the plural society analysts is in the end principally descriptive and open-ended. For example, in the 1960s and 1970s, under the banner of the plural society paradigm, lively and politically charged conferences on Africa were convened.[3] But as the resulting collections of essays show clearly, any number of 'aspects' of possible pluralism (cultural, political, structural) were brought under consideration with no agreed limits to the paradigm. This relative incoherence meant that no firm conclusions were reached about such important issues as whether pre-1980s South Africa could be classified as being a plural society or not, and what followed politically from such classification. Consequently, the ample notion of the plural society comfortably encompassed both searing critiques and thinly veiled apologies for the apartheid state.

Smith's tighter approach stands out in this company, and it also clearly draws to an extent upon Marxist theories of imperialism and global exploitation. Pluralism continues to act chiefly as a category of *institutional* analysis only, referring exclusively to the 'conditions of collective incorporation in the public domain'.[4] To that extent, Smith's approach is consistently 'politicist', even when showing how 'structural pluralism' centrally involves the distribution of material resources in plural societies. Not only is Smith wary of *economic* reductionism here, he is quite intent on avoiding reductionisms of any other sort too – that is, analyses which hinge social plurality around any *single* variable, however important that variable might be (be it 'race', ethnicity, religion, language, or part of the globe). By the same token, in taking this stand the plural society genre commits itself to analytical 'multi-factorialism'. In that vein, Smith declares finally that pluralism itself is a plural, 'multi-dimensional condition' which 'varies in its structure, divisions, and intensities in different societies and in different sections or segments of the same society'.[5] Conceived in this way, pluralism can sometimes refer to cultural differentiation, but sometimes not; in some situations pluralism entails structural domination, but in others it does not.

With this kind of inner hesitancy – flexibility, if you prefer – in evidence, the plural society literature left itself open to a strong critique coming from the 'new' sociologists of race relations and colonialism in the 1970s.[6] Far from exemplifying a critical alternative to liberal pluralist orthodoxies, it was argued, the cruder plural society authors simply articulated the hopes of colonial adminstrators that somehow the workings of the free market would lead to healthy cultural coexistence rather than endemic conflict. In any case, integration into the modernist society of liberal capitalism was expected, one way or the other, to come about. In the more complex analyses, the driving institutionalism seemed to critics continually to tie theory into the perceptions and expectations of the participating social segments of the plural society, and thus into the process of negotiating common ground amongst the diverse value perspectives.

The 'logic' and 'history' of these institutional configurations must be examined on a much wider canvas however, the radicals maintained. Above all perhaps, the *class* relations of colonial societies were not fully graspable when perceived in terms of the clash or convergence of cultural understandings and their institutional expressions. This critique of the plural society literature clearly bears the stamp of the 70s, and its manifest force led to the demise of the plural society paradigm. As in other fields of debate, pluralism came to be seen as flabby and reformist, needing to be replaced by something more rigorous and revolutionary.

That critique still packs a punch. Yet today, in a theoretical climate in which any attempt at structural analysis is liable to be viewed as 'reductionist', and in which 'emancipatory' rhetoric is viewed sceptically, a partial recovery of the defeated paradigm makes some sense. First, now that the insights of a class-theoretic account of 'developing societies' are very well established, it seems appropriate to point out that the institutional fabric of *any* given social formation does after all constitute a specific level of inter- action and analysis, irreducible to whatever more global telos one wishes to postulate as ultimately constraining local options. In that spirit, if the notion of the 'plural society' manages to tap important organizational aspects of late and post-colonial polities, then arguably that is an intrinsically valuable contribution. One of the general points to be made in this context is that to perceive institutional forms exclusively in terms of structurally 'given' or always *imposed* characteristics is to risk underplaying the *consti- tutive* role that cultural beliefs and expectations play in precisely 'instituting' any durable political format. Even if it can persuasively be shown that a global, monistic economic-technological telos is at work (notably 'imperialism'), all the more reason perhaps to identify local variations and openings for resistance to that global ordering.

Third, certain features and problems of the plural society that were thought distinctive of the colonial situation have become manifestly urgent issues within the metropolitan capitalist heart- lands themselves, and in the post-colonial configuration more generally. Above all, extensive labour migration from the less developed to the more developed nations is dramatically transform- ing the social and political character of typically western institutions and attitudes. As the former imperial societies slip into various syndromes of long-term decline, their white, prosperous, liberal self-image becomes but a pale and inadequate reflection of the new, plural, turbulent sociological situation they now encounter on their doorstep. Amongst other things, this changing sociocultural terrain has generated fresh intellectual resources, such as the emerging critical pluralist tendency in academic geography, which concerns itself far more than the older plural society model did, with the *inequalities* of ethnic pluralism, and with the differential politics and identity of *place*.[7]

There is also the spectrum of concerns around 'the politics of difference' in post-colonial societies, something I have touched upon in the previous chapter and which I will be addressing again later. In the meantime, it is worth noting the return to a radicalized 'plural society' model, particularly in states containing distinctive indigenous peoples and movements. In nations such as New Zealand, Canada and Australia, for example, the politicized sections of traditional peoples have deployed with some success a 'plural society' strategy, the idea being that aspects of the cultural separatism of that model can be retained, but *not* its resultant colonial deference and exploitation. The idea is that original peoples, especially when 'advanced' liberal capitalism has so visibly failed them in socioeconomic terms, have a democratic *claim of right* to collective resources, and moreover have a claim to the extra-ordinary recognition and protection of their cultural autonomy.[8] The range of political consequences of this assertion of the rights of First Nations is of course variable and keenly debated. One contender is straightforward separatism. An even tougher proposal is that the original peoples should control their nation, regardless of ethnic proportionality in the population. The principles of 'consociational democracy' would provide for more moderate possibilities, implying as those principles do some degree of separate legislatures, high-level coalition government by the leaders of the different cultural sections, mutual vetoes, and considerable devolved powers of cultural policy and asset management.[9]

In discussions around these options, it is seldom entirely clear whether the prevailing liberal democratic framework is expected to cope with, or collapse under, the proliferation of specific measures such as the 'franchising' to community bodies of previously centralized services such as health and education, or the institution of parallel systems of justice to promote a positive sense of cultural difference. Generally speaking, though, it is the purpose and contribution of the new plural society framework to portray liberal principles as a transient and inadequate historical type of sociopolitical regulation which must adapt and change if it is to survive. Most certainly, for advocates of the radically plural society, liberal democracy is not, as its apologists believe, a universally and eternally valid civic code.

Whether it be in the attempt to develop just solutions to the historical problems of settler societies, or in the effort to create better theories of social identity and division, or simply in the important business of mapping the reasons for the eruption of violent white racism in Europe in the 1980s and 1990s, the old 'plural society' concept thus provides clues as to the possible futures of post-colonial, post-liberal and multicultural states.[10] It takes no more than casual reflection on the serious problems confronting democratic South Africa, for example, where a liberal democratic formula has been implemented for what remains in key respects a plural society, to confirm the continuing relevance of pluralist analysis in that tradition.

III

It will be clear from the last discussion that the fortunes of *legal pluralism* are similar to those of the plural society tradition. Intriguingly, though, the former label also takes us right back to the Continental pluralists in philosophy and law. Recall for example how English political pluralism took from jurists such as Gierke and Maitland the suggestion that corporations had a 'real' existence and so should be recognized in law as full entities.[11] The point here was not simply to alter aspects of the law as such. Rather, the concern was to argue that 'corporations', or 'associations' more generally, reflected the actual *group* life-forms of modern society. This outlook cut right against the dominant liberal assumption that society comprised a mass of *individuals*, who were then coordinated and protected by the might of the centralized *nation state*. Liberal ontology therefore contained only two sorts of social entities that were 'real' – individuals and states.

Just as the English political theorists' associational pluralism attempted to break up this dichotomous social philosophy – and in so doing break the stranglehold of the state itself – so legal pluralism developed as a distinct undercurrent in the sociology of law and in social anthropology, with the express aim of challenging the orthodoxy that the only sort of legitimate law in modern society is state law, and that its only recipients were individuals. Particularly notable in formulating this wider project of legal pluralism was the Austrian sociologist and jurist Eugen Ehrlich, yet another key pluralist figure writing early in the twentieth century.[12] Ehrlich consistently emphasized that lying behind, and theoretically prior to, the facade of state law was *living law*, a complex but very real matrix of rule-governed practices and prohibitions without which no ordinary social relationships could cohere at all. In its full sociological sense, for Ehrlich, law should be understood as the self-regulation of civic associations – families, religious orders, trade unions, occupational clubs, ethnic groups, businesses, leisure associations and so on. Now, as with Figgis, in this picture it is quite necessary for the central state to act as the final source of order, and to set the coordinates of associational interaction. But for Ehrlich and for all subsequent legal pluralists, it is imperative to continually seek to demystify statist ideology, and in particular the metaphysical dogma that state law is *The* Law. This dogma is then readily countered by reference to the amazing range, vitality and order of associational or living law.

Ehrlich's intervention chimed in well with a familiar aspiration amongst social anthropologists: the concern to tap the 'folkways' and autonomous orderings of distinctive cultures, whether bounded by nation states or not. These tracks of legal pluralism came together under the plural society masthead. The late colonial adminstrators as we saw, recognized cultural difference to an extent, and so realized that liberal individualist laws could not be directly imposed on societies in which there might be a number of different but equally strong and legitimate traditional 'legal' norms in operation. Yet, predominantly, an 'assimilationist' prospect was canvassed; sooner or later, led by the market, industrial capitalist ways of life would prevail, and deeply segmented plurality together with its separate folkways would gradually disappear. Arguably, this mere recognition of the existence of folk law amounted only to a 'weak' legal pluralism, a paradigm which actually might be assisting in the incorporation and thus the taming of non-colonial law and community justice, by accepting the overarching validity of bourgeois liberal forms.[13]

Against that background, a 'strong' version of legal pluralism has developed, and it represents two things. First, it is a 'properly' academic effort to tell it like it is, to reveal what is really going on in societies, outside the blinkers of dominant state ideologies. Second, legal pluralism is in part an effort to defend threatened and ignored cultures in the name of political self-determination. Interestingly, as in the plural society tradition more generally, strong legal pluralism draws on a certain socialistic and anti-imperialist theory and practice, and yet the finger is sometimes pointed at Marxism itself as in a sense conspiring with liberal capitalism against Third World populations. This is because both the dominant ideology and its official opposition see the market, and capitalist society generally as inevitably exercising complete domination over alternative cultural practices within its global domain. In that way, 'monocausal descriptions and explanations of law' are reaffirmed in a powerful way.[14] By sharp contrast, legal pluralists imagine the social world as much more variegated and contestable than in either liberalism or Marxism.

We see, then, that legal pluralists have been significantly concerned with traditional cultures and 'underdeveloped' societies. One reason for resuscitating Ehrlich, however, is to remind us that legal pluralism can also be a perspective on contemporary and developed nations too. As radical development theorists and academic anthropologists returned from fieldwork to the politics of diversity within their own home base (usually a western metropolitan setting), it became clear that legal pluralism could be 'applied' just as readily to the central liberal-democratic formations. After all, not only does the state promulgate laws and sanctions: so do universities, political parties, stock exchanges, sporting federations, youth clubs and charities. Moreover, even within state law, there are often strong remnants of customary law. Not only that, it has been a prominent trend within liberal capitalist societies to move strikingly towards 'informalizing' state jurisdiction in areas such as criminal justice and social provision. 'Living law' in the advanced countries is therefore possibly just as rich as it is in exotic cultures, and for any given 'semi-autonomous societal field', there is likely to be a corresponding set of rules and prohibitions.[15]

There are some weighty arguments to be made against legal pluralism, whether in its strong or weak form.[16] One is a recurrent anti-pluralist theme; once the 'boundary' condition of state law is removed, where does legal pluralism stop? Clearly, once that boundary is crossed, the very idea of 'law' quickly disappears into a potentially endless melange of customs, practices, subcultural norms, and rule-governed behaviour of any type whatsoever. 'Law' is what we encounter and re-create whenever we make commodities, go to school, bring up children, play sport, join clubs, and so on. This is an extraordinarily fuzzy and indeterminate kind of pluralism, and it would seem to have no obvious rationale outside critical polemic against mindless statism. Once, perhaps, it was effective in that regard, but nowadays it is fairly commonplace in political sociology to point to the considerable porosity and malleability of state law, and to the contradictions and dislocations between different aspects of the state apparatus in the advanced societies.

Second, there is a kind of 'romanticism' involved in defending other cultures, especially ones with important premodern residues. Now, in many ways this is a noble and defensible task. Yet it is also true that today state law, however incomplete and contested, is clearly the dominant form of regulation in the vast majority of societies and nations. Indeed, it is often only through state law 'exceptions' and enablements that forms of customary law are tolerated and fostered. The demands of accuracy and realism require, then, that if legal pluralism exists, it can hardly be treated in clean separation from state law, nor can it be sustained that there is an approximate equivalence in state-directed and non-state 'legality'.

A final twist in the tale is worth noting, for it parallels many of our other stories of pluralism's development. The critical, antiimperialist phase of legal pluralism tended to posit an 'essentialized' alternative reality and politics. Folkways, everyday normative patterns, assertions of 'real' community justice are baseline categories of legal pluralism that were defined and defended as against the fake universality, and the false 'reality', of bourgeois state law. But now a 'third phase' of legal pluralism has emerged, and it is characterized by *postmodernist* ideas.[17] This style of legal pluralism has it that the subject positions of juridical discourse are the products of shifting and complex *rhetorical constructions*. Where there is 'law', in other words, there is a constructed 'subject' of law, kitted out with ascribed properties, rights and obligations, according to the general nature of the defining legal discourse, or according to the appropriate social microsphere that the discourse addresses.

Both generally and in the particular sociolegal domains, there is an ongoing ideological battle for hegemony amongst the (many) legal subjectivities that are projected. Now, whilst this provocative development certainly continues to undercut the assumptions of statist and bourgeois legal discourse, it also undermines radical legal pluralist alternatives. For one thing, in the postmodern view, strong legal pluralism turns out to be merely the 'Other' of liberal statism. That is, it simply reverses the priorities of universalism, and so in a strange way remains quite dependent on the orthodoxy just to get its oppositional categories going.

Postmodernist legal pluralism would also take issue with the

'realist' basis of strong legal pluralism. This is because the supposedly 'real' multiple folkways that state law ignores, or the
'community justice' that might better serve popular order, are
themselves eminently discursive and shifting constructions: they
construct an image of law's subject and law's domain. Of course
some people, including social scientists, believe that real social life
amongst the people suffering under universal bourgeois state law *is*
cast in that image. That is just the point however - the 'reality effect'
of powerful discursive constructions! The counter-radicalism of
postmodern jurisprudence is thus to say that as analysts we need to
be sceptical of any single claim to uniquely identify the 'reality',
'indigeneity' and 'alternity' beneath the range of discursive legal
images. That kind of search is simply misconceived. This critique of
naive pluralism still remains pluralist itself, it should be said,
because the postmodern legal subject has any number of possible
discursive articulations.[18]

A critique of postmodern pluralism is outlined at several other
points in this book. Here I simply want to reiterate that although
particular variants of legal pluralism have come and gone in its long
history, and whilst serious objections to any version that claims
privileged status can be delivered, legal pluralism does continue to
generate insights, and in some ways those insights are more relevant
now than they were, say, 20 years ago. This is because in key ways
the history, boundaries and legitimacy of the western nation state
are being put into question as never before. For example, a
profound *internationalization* of rights, statutes and regulations is
going on today, accommodating not only economic and military
changes in capitalist relations, but also matters of humanitarian
concern and 'cultural safety' for threatened mores. At the same
time, a considerable process of intra-state devolution of power and
authority is under way. These changes do not at all mean that the
nation state or state law are somehow 'finished', but neither are they
comprehensible without some developed notion of legal pluralism.

IV

The final current of *soi-disant* pluralism that I want to depict has its
academic home in the University of Chicago, from which setting
significant efforts have been made to reshape American literary
theory and philosophy. Perhaps most conspicuously, the Chicagoan

brand of pluralism has been identified with the discourse of the journal *Critical Inquiry*. However, far from being restricted to the business of reading literature in any restricted sense, the driving themes of this pluralism also preoccupy theoretical workers in many other areas of the human sciences. Essentially, the key issues raised are 'the question of general theory' and, relatedly, 'the politics of interpretation'. The favoured self-designation of the literary-cultural pluralists now under review is 'critical pluralism', but having used this label to describe a rather different political science strand of research, I will use the term 'interpretative pluralism' here instead.

Interpretative pluralism has been characterized as having three generations of torchbearers.[19] The first grouping are the well-known first-generation inheritors of William James's pragmatist legacy: John Dewey, George Herbert Mead, the 'Chicago School' sociologists and others. The second grouping, spanning roughly the period from 1940 to 1965, features the philosopher Richard McKeon and the literary critics Kenneth Burke and R.S. Crane, with philosophical allies ouside Chicago in the shape of C.I. Lewis and Stephen Pepper. Nowadays we have a third cohort of Chicago pluralists, headed by the literary critics M.H. Abrams and Wayne Booth, the latter founding *Critical Inquiry*.

One main feature of this brand of pluralism is that, unsurprisingly perhaps, it pays particular intention to the bearing of *literary form* on the substance and political resonance of cultural texts.[20] The nature of the 'text' in question here, we should note, is not restricted to the realm of literature in any canonical sense. In *World Hypotheses* (1942) for example – a book which has certainly been influential for literary theory, but which is unclassifiable in standard disciplinary terms – Stephen Pepper sought to show how a matrix of generic explanatory styles could be used to appraise a wide variety of interpretative visions. Drawing in part upon Pepper's four main analytic categories – formism, mechanism, contextualism, and organicism – Hayden White subsequently developed an account of the master strategies within grand narratives of historical explanation.[21] White's contribution has in turn exercised a strong influence upon theoretical historiography, extending the reach of discursive analysis and 'pluralist' methodological issues still further.[22]

In discussing the range of available strategies in the interpretative process, and in considering the grounds for the merits and 'rightness' of any particular explanatory strategy, interpretative pluralism also had at the forefront of its attention the earnest question, what are the public responsibilities of general cultural pundits? The second main feature of pluralist criticism in this mould is thus its embrace of the *politics* of cultural criticism, and its obsession with just those dilemmas experienced by politically-inclined pluralists in the other fields we have discussed. Does the acceptance and enhancement of interpretative plurality, for example, rule out right and wrong, the possibility of better or worse interpretations? Is *relativism* a responsible interpretative practice (even if it seems an ineluctable theoretical conclusion)? Might not pluralism itself perhaps turn out to be just one more coercive, 'closed' ideology? Are deconstructionist, poststructuralist and postmodernist strategies to be considered pluralist, or are they actually *anti*-pluralist in terms of their methods and goals? These have been some of the tough issues posed within interpretative pluralism.

In his emblematic text of this genre, Wayne Booth unapologetically affirms methodological pluralism, yet also states his hope that the 'nihilistic' spectre of 'anything goes' relativism can be kept at bay. Booth characterizes interpretative monism – his chief target – as the effort 'to discover and proclaim the one truth, sometimes with a tolerant incorporation of fragments from other claimants, often with a total rejection of all other views'.[23] At the same time, unprincipled eclecticism is to be avoided, says Booth, since this prohibits brave theorizing and passionate cultural engagement. Instead, the preferred pluralism must represent a full and generous 'methodological perspectivism'.[24] The idea here is that the integrity and thus the belief-worthiness of monistic understandings should be respected without dilution – except that a range of plausible monisms must be fairly considered and compared.

In this approach, it is not the perspectival *coherence* of monistic interpretative models that is questioned, but rather their *objectivism* and *exclusivism*. Marxism, for example, might be entirely respected for its structural, historical account of the sequence of bourgeois literary forms, and for its critique of literary criticism as ideology. For pluralists, however, the sectarian terms within which Marxist criticism is sometimes voiced is harder to cope with. This is partly because, whilst liberals are in Booth's view (rightly) expected to accept something of the Marxist position, it seems much more difficult for Marxists to be minimally self-critical in return. Alternatively, take deconstruction. Deconstructionism hinges around the thesis that language is inherently unstable and that its textual meanings are undecideable. Now in one sense these are eminently, rigorously pluralist propositions, having the effect of turning all articulations of the True and the Right into contestable constructions only. Though the ends of deconstruction are definitely pluralistic, however, its intellectual means and combative style bear the marks of monistic dogmatism, according to Booth, since deconstructors tend to pile insult upon ridicule in their exposure of the supposed illusions spun by alternative interpretative practices. Yet surely, if they are to be true to their pluralist tenets, deconstructors have no warrant to adopt such a definitive, sectarian mode?[25]

It is the alleged freedom of deconstruction indiscriminately to maraud and to scoff that prompts theorists like Booth to declare themselves 'critical' pluralists rather than outright relativists or poststructuralists. The idea is to try to impose *some* critical limits upon the range of acceptable strong perspectives, using as tough a criteria of consistency and adequacy as comes to hand. Unable consistently to occupy the monistic or relativistic modes of enquiry, but willing to acknowledge their contributions to the interpretative process, interpretative pluralism in this way strives to chart a responsible middle way between the apparent extremes.

There are probably two main lines of attack on interpretative pluralism. The first would begin by pointing out that, strictly speaking, pluralism ought to go all the way down. That is to say, once monism has been abandoned, there just is no 'principled' way of excluding all comers. There is no substantive position which 'splits the difference' between interesting contenders, because if eclecticism is ruled out, that new position must itself be conceived as being just another quasi-monistic effort to reimagine the whole domain under investigation. Not only that, there is no way of legislating for the validity of particular rhetorical styles or modes of combat either. Booth's protest against the 'dangers' and irresponsibility of deconstructionism and relativism must therefore fail by the standards of 'genuine pluralism',[26] since the latter could not deny the rights of any interpretative style, however intractable it may be, simply on account of its apparent unreasonableness. It follows that 'reasonable' interpretative pluralism for its part is confronted with this serious dilemma: either it has to significantly compromise its apparent tolerance of multiple positions, or it must forgo its attempt to police the limits of interpretative practice.

The second main criticism is aimed at 'exposing' the hidden ideological leanings of interpretative pluralism, in much the same way as the unacknowledged 'bias' of pluralist political science was subject to sustained exposure.[27] Despite its professed critical attitude towards apologetic liberalism, the charge is that interpretative pluralism 'backs off' from substantive monism only to fight a rearguard action against nonconformist currents like deconstructionism, asking everyone to be mutually understanding with one another. With this move, arguably, it duplicates precisely the kind of liberal pluralist ideology that is still overwhelmingly dominant in the public realm in the United States.[28] The ideological result of pluralism in both cases, according to this line, is nothing less than an exercise in 'repressive tolerance'. This is because, in the end, the only doctrines that are excluded from reasonable consideration are those which themselves are unreasonable and exclusivist in form – judged according to pluralist lights.

Another unacknowledged dogma of pluralism which becomes evident in polemical exchanges around interpretation, is that the term 'dogma' itself (once, as it happens, a proud label connoting principled engagement and moral fibre) is uniformly taken by pluralists to be a bad thing, and as such, dogma is something that only others profess, never oneself. So for all the generous talk about the passionate, luminous intensity characterizing monistic interpretations (Marxism, feminism, Judaism, Islam, postmodernism, whatever), these world-views must nevertheless all be assumed by pluralists to be in the business of *free and equal discursive exchange*, signatories to what one commentator calls an intellectual ethics of 'general persuasion'.[29] As such, pluralists expect strong discourses to entertain and respect counter-criticism, to 'agree to differ', to abide by the rules of fair play and mutual respect, and in that way minimally uphold the very process of rational appraisal itself. There is an expectation here that the holders of perspectives, the subjects of critical discourse, are subject to fair exchange of views prior to being subject to the particular perspectives that they militantly profess. But the problem with this is that holders of distinctive, driven interpretative perspectives do not particularly *want* to trade their views and visions even-handedly. They argue that this liberal feat of reasonableness is neither achievable nor desirable. Monistic perspectives, in other words, are just not amenable to the kind of sweet reasonableness beloved of pluralists. Theoretical articulation, in other words, is not so much an exercise in liberal reader-persuasion; it is a matter of identity attainment and social combat.

That kind of consideration undoubtedly exposes some of the 'dogmas' and conundrums of moderate pluralism. It suggests, paradoxically, that in order to achieve what Hayden White calls 'genuine pluralism', that is a true embrace of the powers of alternative visions and methods, something of the uncompromising rigour of monism itself must be adopted in order to steel the pluralist temperament. Perhaps that is why writers such as Booth are uncomfortable about deconstructionism; its pluralizing rigour appears to have no ultimate value-base, and yet it does not hesitate to pillory any attempt to establish procedural protocol or final meaning in literary discourse.

The critique of reasonable interpretative pluralism that I have just rehearsed is sharp and persuasive. This critique of liberal pluralist orthodoxy faces a conundrum of its own, however. Despite a considerable degree of 'outsider' and 'activist' posturing in the anti-liberal arguments just portrayed, the authorial conventions of reader persuasion, internal consistency and a commitment to rational (not mortal) combat are surely, as a matter of fact, conformed to by the vast majority of cultural critics, not only moderate pluralists, but theoretical deconstructors, post-modernists, Marxists, and feminists as well. If pluralist norms were *not* subscribed to, books and careers dedicated to the 'exposure' of pluralism would simply not get produced in the stylistic forms and within the social circles that they do.

Moreover, the 'full' or 'genuine' acceptance of relativism is still an eminently 'liberal' ethical move. When we assert that the feeble pluralist cannot truly understand the white heat of the truly non-pluralist vision, the assumption must be that, by contrast, the passionate 'genuine' pluralist *does* in some deep way have access to the separatist logic and verve of the various incommensurable paradigms. Yet it is extremely unlikely that your average passionate pluralist/relativist actually does subscribe to, far less *lives*, any one of these monistic visions, particularly in a climate currently very hostile to totalizing schemas and unreflexive commitments. The dilemmas of pluralism are thus dilemmas which confront all pluralists, not just liberal academic pluralists. Even in the anti-pluralist case where someone gives allegiance to a given monism, it might still seem no bad idea to try to draw others away from rival perspectives by convincing them of the advantages of one's own position. We give intellectual allegiance to a particular perspective, and to it alone, partly because it is believed to show explanatory and affective superiority over other perspectives. Short of a belief in spontaneous conversion, it cannot be only a 'liberal' pluralist strategy to seek to demonstrate those advantages in a reasoned way, with an agreed agenda of issues and cases.

V

The survey of pluralist lineages and debates that I have conducted in the last two chapters has inevitably been somewhat selective and condensed. But no survey of pluralism could be adequate without consideration of at least that handful of currents that I have identified and begun to critically evaluate. At a time when pluralist strategies and values are being invoked and exemplified as never before, it is necessary to have a sense of the richness, diversity and yet also the common ground amongst the various subspecies of the category. Part of that common ground, as we have seen latterly in this chapter, is constituted by a number of difficult problems and possible solutions in the field of interpretative methodology. It is to the further consideration of these methodological problems and solutions that I turn next.

Expressions of
Methodological
Pluralism

I

Questions of methodology and epistemology have always troubled
– some would say have always plagued – the social sciences. One
after another, various models of scientific explanation have been
imported from the philosophy of natural science and used to gauge –
some would say to police – the credentials of general theories and
substantive research programmes in the social disciplines. From the
very beginning, each of these models and the general founding idea
of scientificity in the study of society have been challenged by the
'interpretative' underside of the Enlightenment tradition. Today,
that debate between quasi-scientific objectivism and anti-scientistic
interpretivism is still, as we have already seen, very much alive. In
what is often characterized as our 'post-positivist' methodological
condition today, it is increasingly accepted both that a diversity of
valid philosophies, paradigms, general theories, approaches to
research, and value orientations exist, and that it is neither possible
nor desirable to say definitively which amongst these are more
objective, true, scientific, or essential. That broad outlook is what I
am calling 'methodological pluralism', and in this chapter I want to
analyse something of how it came about, its different expressions
within social scientific metatheory, and some of the problems it
faces.

The once-dominant 'positivist' – it would be more accurate to say
'logical empiricist' – explanatory format for the social sciences was

an impressively crafted attempt to place our theoretical aspirations in line with those of the natural sciences conceived in a certain way. Unfortunately, being notoriously less 'mature', and dealing with a few more imponderables than physics, social scientists were regarded by the logical empiricists as destined to produce, at best, imperfect explanations. Instead of the fully fledged 'covering laws' which the theoretical structures of the 'proper' sciences would generate in order to interpret their systematic observations, the social sciences for their part could only produce 'explanation sketches' to make sense of their empirical material. According to Carl Hempel, one of the chief architects of the 'covering law' or 'hypothetico-deductive' method, that was actually a fair achievement in the circumstances. We should not be too disappointed.[1]

Many students of human interaction *did* take offence at their proposed second-rate intellectual citizenship however, and so a particularly strong resurgence of interpretivism broke out during the 1960s. It was argued that the social sciences were simply not to be compared with the natural sciences; that the causal order and deductive logic of positivism just did not apply in our province; that a more hermeneutic and 'internal' relationship held between the theoretical apparatuses and the subject–objects of the humanities and social sciences. That response seemed to register well enough some of the things that were distinctive about the human sciences. Then it was asked further: what if the *natural sciences themselves* do not fit the logical empiricist model? In that case, ironically, the humanists may have given science away altogether to the enemy in order to protect the precious uniqueness of the human subjects we study.

Accordingly, through the 1960s and 1970s, attempts were made to avoid the extremes of positivist scientism and humanist 'exceptionalism'. One general strategy was to try to reconceive the whole idea of science itself, in particular to reconceive the relationship within it between theory and observation, and to look again at the status of science's real entities. Repeated through many commentaries, it became commonplace to assert both that, contrary to positivism, all observations are 'theory-laden', and that all theories are 'underdetermined' by the available evidence. This new orthodoxy led to a much more fluid, less algorithmic conception of the forms of knowledge that the sciences – both natural and human – produce.

By 'softening' somewhat the notion of scientific explanation in this way, some writers thought it still possible to reunite the social with the natural sciences as equally noble and quasi-objective endeavours, in spite of their manifest differences. The whole movement of 'structuralism' was just such a concerted effort to blast a viable, coherent way between positivism and humanism. In addition, a rich succession of other sophisticated post-empiricist philosophies of science found a home in texts dealing with the object and method of the social sciences: for example, Karl Popper's notion of science as moving forward through a dialectic of conjecture and refutation; Thomas Kuhn's account of scientific development as a sequence of incommensurable paradigms; Imre Lakatos's formulation of the logic of the 'scientific research programme'; Larry Laudan's idea that science works through problem-solving; and Roy Bhaskar's 'realist' account of the 'open' texture of the social and natural objects of science, featuring various real but unmanifest 'generative mechanisms' and virtual structures.[2]

Whilst militantly recommending the goodness of science for social science, these new philosophies and their offshoots accepted to a far greater extent than logical empiricism that science was in fact a human and social product. As such, its 'objectivity', though still theoretically desirable and to varying degrees achievable, was intrinsically provisional and uncertain. The producers of science, moreover, were recognized to be very much *social* actors, firmly located in a particular culture and history. Now once you accept (a) the theory-ladenness of observation, (b) the cultural specificity of theory, and (c) the necessary impermanence of the scientific knowledge so produced, it becomes very difficult to rescue much at all of the lofty idea of scientific objectivity. Popper formulated a typically tough and straightforward response to the slide towards relativism that ensued. The constraining power of our governing theoretical or cultural frameworks for knowledge, he argued, has been seriously exaggerated. As social actors, we are of course influenced by our situation and values, but as individuals we are never wholly imprisoned within any single cell of interpretation, and even less so is science, when taken as a whole. Indeed, whilst science may be, definitively, the product of the human imagination, its results, once achieved, can be seen as 'migrating' to another sort of world, a 'world three' of enduring and objective (if ever-incomplete) ideas.[3]

Take or leave the Popperian terminology, something like that argument has remained at the heart of the opposition to relativism ever since. Understandably perhaps, many social scientists are sceptical of the cognitive idealism it involves. Such scepticism found perhaps its most substantively promising expression in the development of a 'strong programme' in the sociology of knowledge through the 1970s and 1980s.[4] The idea here was that scientific developments could be best analysed as expressions of the *social interests* of the principal groups who moulded the cultural institutions of science. Traditional philosophical idealists are of course bound to be offended by this type of sociologism, because it seems to demean science; the content of knowledge is somehow subordinated to its social functions, which are then allegedly exaggerated out of all proportion. Also, evidently, *relativism* gets taken for granted, and this seems to leave scientific knowledge on a par with any other system of cultural and political belief.

In terms of the self-esteem of *social* science, however, the new sociology of science was nothing less than liberating, suggesting a rapid promotion of the status of social science itself in the intellectual hierarchy. As with Kuhn's propositions about how dominant paradigms get established within the occupational cultures of scientists, instead of being philosophically dictated to by explanatory models taken from physics, natural science itself gets reconceived in terms of its own social organization, ideologies, and material interests.

Refreshing though the strong programme's challenge to traditional science and philosophy was, it has never been wholly clear just how central epistemological relativism is to that challenge – or if it is, whether that matters. In fact, the strong programmers were careful to say that the truth or otherwise of beliefs was not really their problem, only that the ascendancy of true (scientific) as well as less systematic (ideological) beliefs could be shown to have a social rationale. In that case, however, whilst reference to the social may help explain why certain beliefs come to be dominant, something else must explain why scientific beliefs are generally truer (if they are truer) than other forms of belief. Put that way, the strong programme represents not so much a (relativist) position within epistemology as a rigorous abstention from matters epistemological.

This type of hesitancy within the relativistic and sociological approach to scientific knowledge has encouraged other sorts of non-empiricist philosophers to continue to run with the idea that whilst science is in some ways socially determined, in other ways it is not. According to Bhaskar's scientific realism, for example, scientific theories are conceived as always having both a 'transitive' (social) and an 'intransitive' (natural or transcendental) dimension, such that the one cannot after all be reduced to the other. That sort of flexible realist response then in turn attracted considerable support amongst radical social scientists in the 1970s and early 1980s, and ensured that the post-empiricist commitment to methodological pluralism remained at a fairly general and vague level. By this time, the bottom line in pluralism seemed to be the possibly innocuous claim that the social sciences have their own distinct objects and methods of study.[5]

The development of, and variations within post-empiricist thinking were happening largely prior to and independently of 'postmodernism' and its precursor poststructuralism. Yet there can be little doubt that the mounting challenge not only to positivism but to *any* type of 'foundationalism' within sociophilosophical discourse (including realism) was accelerated dramatically as the term postmodernism spread outwards from its original location in aesthetics and architecture. Under its masthead, the familiar boundaries between philosophy and other disciplines, between Continental and Anglo-American traditions, and between substantive and methodological reflection became significantly blurred.

These trends were reflected within mainstream philosophy of science, with influential writers such as 'anarchist' Paul Feyerabend, 'soft-realist' Hilary Putnam, and 'creationist' Nelson Goodman explicitly labelling their orientations as 'pluralist'.[6] Adjacently, other analytical philosophers were enthusiastically confessing that the very notion of scientific explanation was once again entirely up for grabs, now that the last vestiges of positivism had gone.[7] In that kind of context, the view quickly develops that Theory should no longer be seen as what correct theories deliver when they objectively map the real world; rather, theories are best seen as shifting vocabularies of insight and zones of engagement. Explanation, in other words, is not really 'about' achieving truth and validity as such at all, but is rather a mode of engaging *other people* about some of the things we find interesting and important.[8]

With postmodernism in command today, the attack on foundationalism involves an assault on the privileged role that philosophical discourse itself has tended to play in many variants of the western intellectual tradition. As well as choosing freely between various metatheoretical perspectives, postmodern pluralism encourages a move right out of the discourse of intellectual legitimation altogether, stressing instead the affective, ideological, technical, professional, rhetorical and passionate character of our value commitments in theory and practice. For an example of the radical pluralist consequences of this 'archaeological' move in social thought, debates in the sociology of science are again instructive. With the splash made by the 'strong programme' in the sociology of knowledge, the stranglehold of legislative philosophy over our ideas about what constituted 'real' science was apparently broken. Idealism and objectivism were replaced by materialism and relativism as the guiding metamethodological norms. However, in postmodernism generally, there is almost as great a suspicion of 'sociologism' as there is of philosophical imperialism. Sociology, after all, has foundationalist and reductive ambitions. So the worry grows that the monistic idealism of philosophy has been defeated only for us to see erected in its place the equally monistic materialism of sociology. In other words, whilst the content of the enquiry has altered, the attempt to find a formulaic solution to the 'problem' of scientific explanation still persists. Instead of locating that solution in terms of the eternal logic of cognition (rationalist philosophy), it gets located in the logic of the social (the strong programme). Armed with these arguments, and progressively moulding itself to the ironic postmodernist temper, one influential group of authors has sought to drop the label of 'the sociology of scientific knowledge', adopting in its place the far less legislative 'science studies'. This redesignation is shorthand for what has become an ultra-reflexive and multi-factorial analysis of scientific *practice* (rather than theory).[9]

II

In line with that sketch of the recent history and character of pluralist metatheoretical moves, declarations of pluralism are now common within the metadiscourses of the substantive disciplines and within philosophy of social science texts. Right across these genres, value-diversity amongst social scientists is widely acknowledged, and the underdetermination of theories by data is standardly cited, these two theses jointly entailing a necessary plurality of competing theories in all the sciences. It needs to be said, however, that this post-empiricist consensus around pluralism does not take us very far. Typically, after that point of agreement has been reached, closet realist and 'naturalist' authors are inclined to carry on regardless in making their bids *for* science in the social sciences; humanist commentators for their part still emphasize particular interpretative or hermeneutic stances; pragmatists or anarchists launch into an exposure of the grave damage done to concrete social scientific investigation by all types of philosophical formalism.

This latter approach is perhaps the most militantly pluralistic one, setting up a kind of Feyerabendian project for social science. In that mould, Paul Diesing for example states with deliberate paradox that whilst his book on method spends much time deconstructing philosophy as the governing matrix of social methodology, no philosophical conclusions or preferences of any kind follow from his arguments. This is because it is creativity and insight, not truth, that motivate good work in the social sciences. For creativity to emerge, 'a pluralism of conflicting research programmes' must flourish.[10] If social science does happen to produce anything like truth, then what it produces is a 'multiple, contradictory truth for our time'.[11] The point here is not to deny the important role of theories within specific substantive domains, only that these must be judged in terms of their value to their users rather than according to their conformity to some abstract formal model of all explanation. In social philosophy as in the administration of tertiary education generally, the guiding concept of disinterested knowledge acquisition has been supplanted by that of responsiveness to stakeholders' concerns.

Other overviewers of the new, pluralistic philosophy of social science also support a user-friendly approach, and are consequently also critical of formalism, but they feel rather more uncomfortable about the *pragmatism* which inevitably results. James Bohman, for example, forthrightly announces that social science knowledge is practice and value-driven, that the notion of explanatory adequacy is problematic, and that due to the sheer variety of analytical forms and resources available, social science these days just does not require any unifying theories.[12] Accordingly, multiplicity and indeterminacy (and thus pluralism) need to be seen as being at the heart of our methodological situation. Yet rather than leaving things at that, and in effect scratching where it doesn't itch, to use

Richard Rorty's argot, Bohman cannot quite shake off the feeling
that the scientistic idea of explanatory 'rigour' needs to be retained
somewhere in the picture. In that spirit he suggests that common
'standards' of evidence and coherence still have to be adhered to.
Bohman hopes that this concession to tradition will lead to
'adequate and detailed patterns of explanation'.[13] But the problem
here is that for realists and anarchists alike (though they would have
contrary values on the matter), this sort of concession to tradition
would have to be classed as a damaging compromise for pluralism,
because the very language of 'adequacy' and 'explanation' sustains
promises of scientific monism–rationalism, not a more relaxed
pluralist attitude.

The two pluralist approaches I have just reported are rather
different from one another. The first, more radical move, is
tantamount to pragmatism: whatever methodologies and theoretical resources work for you – and you have a wide choice – is fine. Do
not bother yourself about seeking any higher court of appeal. The
second variety is more cautious, and as a result is caught in a
dilemma. There is no 'objective' way of deciding which of the
various competing metaperspectives is best, and yet the tasks of first
considering each seriously, and second attempting an assessment of
their explanatory merits are felt to raise questions of adequacy and
principle that go beyond pragmatic stakeholder-friendliness. In the
light of this difference between pragmatic and cautious pluralists,
the current widespread consensus around methodological pluralism
can only take a limited and negative form: the denial that there is
any 'one proper set of rules' in the study of human behaviour.[14] Put
like that, however, quasi-foundationalists such as philosophical
realists in the social sciences would also be entitled to participate in
the pluralist accord. Realists might say that whilst there are of
course many valid ways of exploring reality, and many partial truths
at any given point in time, it is still rational to presuppose the
existence of one real (complexly structured) reality, and to project
in principle one set of truths for each object domain.

III

Debates within specific disciplinary discourses confirm the idea that
if pluralism is a widespread condition in the social sciences, its

precise demands and implications are far from obvious. In particular, there are a variety of views on whether methodological pluralism is to be taken neat or diluted. We have already seen, for example, how feminist studies reflect the dilemmatic quality of the wider philosophical debates. The experience of ambivalence, of course, is often said to be a constitutive part of our postmodern intellectual condition, and accordingly some feminists, sociologists, and contributors to the cultural studies field have tried to be *positive* about the dilemmas of theoretical pluralism, without suggesting that there is an obvious answer – even a strongly pluralist one.[15]

This predicament can readily be brought out in the cultural studies case, where a myriad texts and departments have sprung up world-wide in a remarkable way since around 1980. Now, with no vested interests in any conventional disciplinary base, spokespeople for cultural studies have openly acknowledged, and made a great virtue of, its theoretical fluidity. Indeed the recent international institutionalization of cultural studies has been launched on the basis that the new discipline is, almost by definition, exploratory, interdisciplinary, vaguely political and methodologically pluralist.[16] There is certainly something in this. At the same time, however, much of the groundwork in the cultural studies tradition was undertaken by individuals and groups (such as the Birmingham Centre for Contemporary Cultural Studies) who were interested in defending an interdisciplinary space and broad political project, *without* succumbing to a bland and all-purpose pluralism.[17] If no single author or paradigm or project ultimately emerged as final orthodoxy, then possible 'solutions' or combinations of solutions were explored with a passion and seriousness that simply does not square with pragmatic or ironic purposes. Even with the post-modernization of cultural studies now reaching saturation point, the discomfort as well as the promise of pluralist ambivalence comes through quite strongly.[18]

Today the supposedly more 'conventional' academic disciplines, especially perhaps sociology, actually share many of the styles of research, topics of investigation and methodological dilemmas of new fields such as cultural studies. The main difference perhaps is simply that an organizational commitment to the very idea of 'the discipline' and its achievements tends to work against the open embrace of ambivalence and identity-crisis. One recurrent means of stabilizing the choice between current options is to produce synthetic rereadings of 'the classics'.[19] (We might note that this conventional practice has already become a standard feature of cultural studies too.) Another strategy is to re-establish the discipline's substantive potential by rigorously dephilosophizing it. Thus without wishing to resurrect straight empiricism, a number of theoretically inclined sociologists have argued that the influence of philosophy itself – including the apparently anti-epistemological postmodernism – on specifically *sociological* theory has been counter-productive. In response, sociological theory ought to be substantively directed rather than purely formal, ought to be of the 'middle-range' sort rather than the social–philosophical sort, and essentially should be a matter of research-oriented conceptual crafting rather than abstract speculation. In this move, a pragmatic turn is recommended as a way of attuning sociologists to plurality without getting them involved in unsolvable questions about whether foundations are necessary or not.[20]

In the USA, a similar urge to put philosophy in the back seat has surfaced with the launching of the label 'metatheory'. A manifesto collection of this new genre has it that metatheorizing is sociology's equivalent to postmodernism, and that as such it constitutes an important counter-move to philosophizing within sociology. Meta-theory in this usage is defined by a 'reflexive awareness of multiplicity' and by its commitment to theoretical pluralism and egalitarianism.[21] In another metatheoretical collection, this one having a more psychological orientation, the editors warmly commend the current theoretical confusion as being entirely productive, with social science research necessarily cast as an exciting hotbed of pluralistic activity.[22]

Three main conundrums face metatheorists of this sort. The first arises when we note that neo-positivist metaperspectives also make an appearance in these collections, which claim, overall, to be *post*-positivist. One way round this obstacle is to accept that, as long as it remains just one rhetorical *option*, perhaps even positivism is acceptable in those terms. To exclude positivism, after all, especially when it appears in suitably humble form as one amongst many, would be to resort once again to legislative theoretical closure. Despite that generosity of spirit, it is unlikely that positivists, or any other sort of fully committed methodologist, would think this a fair reflection of their ambitions, since the whole attraction of positivism has always been that it promises to beat a clear path through the morass of opinions and validity-claims associated with eclecticism and subjectivism.

The second conundrum concerns the nature of those metatheories which, unlike positivism, are designed specifically to reflect at the methodological level the substantive plurality which exists out there in the social sphere itself. Take sociologist Jeffrey Alexander's claim for the metatheoretical status of his notion of 'multi-dimensionality'.[23] This governing term represents an ecumenical attempt to bring together in an inclusive way *all* those theoretical resources which have been theorized excessively monistically in past contributions. The idea is that otherwise competing governing conceptions can be shown to have a partial validity when reconceived as common components of an umbrella methodological label, 'multi-dimensionality'. The problem with this solution is its sheer formalism – as if you just coin the right 'different-but-integrated' label and the competition which has characterized competing paradigms for decades can just be declared over, tamed.

The third conundrum of 'metatheory' emerges when we compare two ideas which can be found in each of the collections I am singling out as emblematic. One pluralistic metatheoretical stance casts itself as *post*-paradigm reflection, while the second claims that metatheory represents the open acceptance of *multiple* paradigms. The second claim is significantly weaker than the first, since it obviously retains the idea of paradigms as a guide to how theories are put together, whereas the first claim is intended to get us beyond the crutch of paradigms entirely. The first implies that 'anything goes' in putting an approach together; the second implies that the various elements of theoretical assessment automatically fall into well-defined packages.

IV

Having looked at how issues of pluralism are at the forefront of the concerns of the philosophy of science and social science, and of disciplines such as cultural studies and theoretical sociology, I want to continue the discussion by making a threefold distinction between technical–methodological pluralism, epistemological pluralism and ontological pluralism. Beginning with the first of these, a very familiar and low-key rendering of methodological pluralism is the idea that in social scientific work we can draw on a wide range of relevant *research methods*. Not so long ago the various *qualitative* methodologies carried a distinctly second-rate status, on the grounds that interpretative forms of investigation did not quite count as being properly scientific. That legacy of positivism is no longer perhaps the orthodoxy, but it does linger on to considerable effect in some of the self-declared 'hard' disciplines of the social sciences and in the judgements of national funding bodies.

Contrary efforts to privilege certain kinds of qualitative analysis have also been undertaken, for example in Marxist claims on behalf of the historical and dialectical interpretation of sources, amongst advocates of 'action research' or ethnomethodological techniques, and in arguments to the effect that feminism has its own special 'mutualist' techniques for investigating women's experiences. Other efforts in methodological closure can be witnessed in the weighty claims that are occasionally made for ethnography or for the 'comparative method', and so on. These exclusivist gestures are perhaps not so popular now as they were in the 1970s and 1980s. For one thing, radical theories have been significantly pluralized in their substantive tenets, and this has had methodological spin-offs. Moreover, many who might once have argued in a methodologically exclusive way are now finding themselves in established academic positions, and there is always a certain pressure towards pluralism in dealing with the different interests, prejudices and teaching preferences of colleagues and research students. Accordingly, the predominant academic view today is probably that your choice of method is relatively open, as long as it is in the end shown to be appropriate to your research goal, is established in the guts of the research problem, and is theoretically glossed in some plausible way.

However, even if that kind of 'pedagogic' pluralism of methods is widespread, pluralism even at this level remains contestable. This is because it is hard to envisage a clean separation of 'technical' methodology from methodology in the sense of the kinds of strategic research question and human values which drive all our specialist studies. It is all very well to advise students of the wide range of methods available, but once we are to our own satisfaction 'inside' a particular project and methodology, it is usually obvious to us that some techniques are 'better' – not just better fitting, but more *valid* – than others at unearthing the things that we have come to see as most important. From that standpoint, it is quite difficult to revert to the bland liberal notion that anyone can study anything about society, and in doing so can freely choose their research techniques. Even though radical standpoints have been diluted somewhat, many social scientists still feel that some kind of 'indissoluble bond' between techniques and theories can and *ought* to characterize innovative programmes. If that attitude holds, the pluralist idea of a neutral menu of available and equal research techniques is undermined to an extent.[24]

A second sense of methodological pluralism refers to the more general idea that there are always a range of available perspectives, approaches, paradigms or conceptual frameworks for theory and research. Possibly just to *recognize* this diversity makes you a kind of pluralist, but probably at a minimum you should not only recognize but also *approve* of methodological diversity in this sense. However, this brand of pluralism is still fairly minimal, and is quite compatible with an ultimately monistic view of truth and reality. Thus one realist philosopher writes that pluralists should be willing:

> to tolerate and utilise a diversity of ideas and approaches, while at the same time acknowledging criteria which afford the possibility of objective comparison and evaluation of the diverse alternatives tolerated and utilised.[25]

This is of course rather contentious. Only the first clause in the statement reflects the kind of 'intuitive' pluralism of many social scientists, which is basically an expression of intellectual liberalism or tolerance. The second clause reflects the author's own rather objectivist inclinations, inclinations that many pluralists find problematical. Still, pluralism clearly has to be firmed up even further if it is to pack a real punch against monism. One way of doing this has been to swap talk of 'approaches' for talk of 'paradigms'. At this point we encounter again the kind of interpretative pluralism discussed at the end of the last chapter. The line from this angle is that you cannot just prowl around eclectically between paradigms; once you have bought into a particular, theorized way of seeing, your interpretative commitment goes all the way down. To be a 'paradigm' pluralist thus involves a full and serious methodological 'perspectivism', such that there are always a number of *distinctive* and *incompatible* interpretative frameworks around from which to choose. And it does less than justice to the integrity of these well-sculpted options simply to raid them opportunistically for partial insights, casually expecting to be able to put the results together in a compelling way. This line of 'non-eclectic pluralism' thus envisages the theoretical scene as being populated by a diversity of strong theories and values, the independent logic and goals of which must be respected.

We have, then, a progression from the belief that intellectual diversity is a good thing, to the claim that there is no definitive interpretative route to objectivity, to the idea that there are always a number of 'valid' rival perspectives. The critical pluralist still does not have to say that 'anything goes', since each paradigm can be addressed in terms of its particular theoretical strengths and weaknesses and in terms of appropriate empirical evidence. Put that way, whilst 'objectivity' might well be a victim of pluralism, 'rationality' need not be; we can properly appraise the claims and values of each perspective in forming our intellectual commitments. However, the matter could be engaged further, because this talk of proper appraisal still seems to hanker romantically after a form of liberal detachment and fair play. Perhaps we should just own up and declare that paradigm commitment does not so much involve a reasonable choice amongst various perspectives as a full-scale clash of 'divergent rationalities'.[26]

V

At this point methodological pluralism can be seen to require epistemological relativism for its support, and vice versa. Without the basic claim that a plurality of very different styles of knowledge always exist, the conclusion that validity is always relative to the particular norms of those different styles could hardly be sustained. 'Serious' or 'genuine' pluralism thus amounts to much the same thing as relativism in this context, and like pluralism, relativism can be couched in terms of variants of increasing strength. One minimal rendition is the argument that claims to science, truth, validity, etc. always emerge from particular schemes of interpretation, and from particular investigative practices. These schemes and practices in turn form part of specific cultural traditions. Thus it can be stated that scientific validity is relative to the subcultural and general values of historical societies. Now, although realists for their part are often taken to be opposed to epistemological relativism, *this* sense of relativism poses no problem for realists, for all that seems to be required here is that science be recognized to be a social practice. Indeed, some realists feel that realism actually *demands* relativism; as transient real creatures, living in a world whose complex generative mechanisms are not usually manifest on the surface of things, it should be obvious that our epistemic perspectives, however complete we try to make them, will only ever have a partial and passing fix on reality. That is simply what it means for us to be part of a wider objective world of variously enduring mechanisms.[27]

A tougher relativist position directly denies what is often claimed to be the basis of any type of 'realism', 'objectivism' or 'absolutism', namely the assumption that we can, through science, attain a 'God's eye view' of reality as it exists 'in itself'. Additionally, contemporary relativists are keen to rebut the 'classic' argument against relativism, namely, that it is self-contradictory. According to that charge, the claim that 'all validity is relative' is itself an *absolute* claim seeking universal authority, and this is actually a contradiction in terms. In response, it is often said that relativism is in the business of *questioning* all absolute claims, not *adding* to them. In any case, relativists are not nearly so bothered as absolutists by the idea of embracing an apparent 'contradiction'. This is because the alternative idea, that knowledge has a status, form and essence that is somehow *beyond* the contradictory aspirations of its human makers is itself mightily contestable and as it happens completely undemonstrable. Relativists today are also inclined to point out that in embracing relativism they have no intention whatsoever of giving up on 'proper' standards of evaluation or comparison. In that spirit they insist that they are not so much *for* something called 'relative truth' as *against* all forms of superhuman absolutism. As anthropologist Clifford Geertz puts it, the position advanced here is not so much relativism as 'anti-anti-relativism'.[28]

In spite of the ingenuity of this 'double negative' formulation, the denial of the ability of human cognitive endeavours to scale the fences of their cultures of origin, does establish a fairly thoroughgoing relativism. Against it stand a number of counter-arguments that are not easily dispelled. The first is the 'Popper problem': that relativism is extremely deterministic, hugely overstating the total constraining power of specific cultural norms and conceptual frameworks. The latter are viewed, implausibly, both as hermetically sealed, and as governing fully and equally the mind-sets of all who work within them. Second, whatever the protests of modest relativists to the contrary, intellectual relativism does lead to a sort of moral 'nihilism'. In other words, without some regulative ideal of cross-cultural, transparadigm validity, the notion of worthwhile intracultural and intercultural critique is hard to sustain. Some postmodernists ask us at this stage to just let go of our obsession with the necessity of 'grounding' critique in this way, pointing to the damage caused to modern societies by an over-serious, ever-ordering intellectual and political culture. That is a salutary reminder. Even so, human life does happen to be, so far and generally speaking, rather serious and ordered; arguably to give up on 'serious' critique would be to abandon our collective fate to the winds of chance and time.

Whether in its modest or thoroughgoing guise, a key proposal of relativism is that no one style of knowledge or interpretation is any more valid, in some objective sense, than any number of alternatives. In spite of the countless efforts by objectivists to refute this idea at a purely philosophical level, probably the most effective response is morally and historically driven. As Ernest Gellner has stated, almost as a simple matter of fact, 'everything about the condition of mankind in our age makes it utterly plain that cognitive relativism is false ... it simply and totally misdescribes our collective situation.'[29]

The point here is that the assumption within relativism that there exists a 'symmetrical' world of equivalent cultures is badly mistaken. On the contrary, the scientific-rationalist style of reasoning has had distinctive and irreversible 'success', even if some awful things have been part of that success. Like it or not, all traditional cultures and all alternative styles of reasoning have been transformed by instrumental rationality and scientific calculation. In the face of that situation, ironic relativism, the product of intellectuals who are 'intoxicated with the idea of plural visions' yet 'feeling guilty about their own cultural privilege' arguably represents a major failure of nerve and judgement.[30]

I find the Gellner-style response to relativism powerful and timely, but I doubt that it can be quite the last word on the matter. After a point, it may not be terribly helpful, for example, to regard scientific rationality as a coherent paradigm all of its own. 'Science', we should remember is a hypostatization, most beloved by western rationalists. Couched in that way, both the intrinsic connections between scientific rationality and liberal market societies, and the 'obviousness' of the supposed internal meaning and logic of 'science' tend to get over-cooked.

VI

Thoroughgoing variants of epistemological pluralism/relativism appear in turn to entail *ontological* pluralism, the final aspect of methodological pluralism that I want to touch upon. It is particularly noticeable in postmodern forms of epistemological pluralism that the notion of 'plural constructions' leads directly to the assertion of 'diverse realities'.[31] Ontological pluralism in this sense has a distinctly 'idealist' cast. If there is no such thing as transperspectival or cross-cultural objectivity, then the question of what the world is like 'in itself' cannot be meaningfully addressed. Instead, there are many *ways* the world is, and indeed it might as well be said that there are as many *worlds* as there are plausible discursive constructions. In terminology derived from Nelson Goodman, we might summarize this stance in the formula: 'many versions, many (constructed) worlds'.[32]

Traditionalists are uncomfortable with the discursive rendering of ontological pluralism. It has already been noted, for example, that some 'realists' refuse to accept that there exists a necessary link between epistemological pluralism and ontological pluralism. They contend that it is only by supposing the independent existence of one real (complex) material world that the plurality of world versions can be properly explained in the first place. The relevant slogan here might be 'many (fragmented, temporary) versions, one (enduring) world'.[33]

A third possibility is to accept *ontological* pluralism, but to reject *epistemological* pluralism. This option has two main thrusts. First, it can be pointed out that conventional realism is very much a 'one world' doctrine. Trouble is rarely if ever taken actually to demonstrate this crucial taken-for-granted belief, however, and on further reflection, the idea that there is one and only one real world is very limited and unsubstantiated. Perhaps it is more appropriate and plausible to speak, literally, of 'many worlds'.[34] The proposition here is that we are not speaking only 'metaphorically' when we talk of the different 'worlds' of, for example, physics and chemistry, the economy and culture, love and science; the unit objects and explanatory processes highlighted in these discourses arguably refer to *different actual orders* of being. Astronomers appear to have no problem in regarding the different planets, or star systems, as different (if connected) worlds, so why should terrestrial and human scientists?

One interesting question for social scientists in following this brand of ontological pluralism is whether 'society' represents one *single* world in the midst of the other natural world-systems, or whether, within the social itself, there are actually a *number* of distinguishable realms of being, each of which deserve to be accorded the status of a separate 'world'. In this spirit, it is increasingly accepted, for example, that discontinuity rather than flat contradiction marks the distinction between 'macro' and 'micro' forms of interaction; between the unconscious and conscious psychic economies; between class and gender systems of stratification, and so on. These different but contiguous realms or spheres or levels of 'society' can seriously be entertained as actual or potential real worlds. Like the substantial number of real worlds which constitute the 'cosmos', the task would then be to try to establish whether a given putative world can be demonstrated to possess relatively autonomous principles of operation and characteristic units of being.

The headline for this third brand of ontological pluralism can be summarized as: 'one (true, valid) version for every single world, but many worlds'. As well as departing from the standard assumptions of one-world realism, this standpoint works against a constructivist and relativist line too. It maintains that each of the many worlds is perfectly *real*, not just imagined, and for each of these worlds there will (eventually or in principle) be only *one* comprehensive valid theory. Of course, at any given point there are likely to be several plausible versions for each of the various worlds, but it is never legitimate to regard all of these versions as equally valid in principle. In this way, interestingly, you can deny strong epistemological pluralism whilst endorsing 'extreme' ontological pluralism.

VII

I have been pushing the notion of methodological or philosophical pluralism to see if it represents a new, single and powerful stance in the metatheory of the sciences/social sciences, and also to see whether it involves an 'anti-realist' outlook. There is no doubt that a strong pluralist climate of opinion can be detected across a number of levels of abstraction. That there is and should be a number of methods to be legitimately drawn upon in social science research; that a number of more general theoretical paradigms usually exist; that there are many valid governing values for our work; that there are divergent rationalities; that there are many versions of the world, and even that there are many real 'worlds': all these claims are pluralist in some sense, and they are also plausible and attractive in various ways.

It can be said with some confidence, then, that there are distinctive pluralist approaches to the metatheory of the social sciences. At the same time, I have identified four main reasons which block a more definitive statement of pluralism in this domain.

1 You can be a pluralist at any *one* of the specified levels, without commitment to pluralism at any (or all) of the others, thus leaving the possibility of a reassertion of a 'monist' option at the point where the preferred pluralism runs out. Thus you can accept a pluralism of technical methodology and embrace a general sense of the value of having a diversity of 'approaches' *without* accepting full-scale 'paradigms' pluralism. You can accept paradigm pluralism without seeing this as necessarily requiring a commitment to 'divergent rationalities'. And you can endorse some version of rationality pluralism/epistemological relativism without embracing ontological pluralism.

2 Within each of my putative 'levels', pluralism comes in a *descriptive* and a *prescriptive* form. It is one thing to say, for example, that a number of research methods exist, and that this makes for a lively scene. But it is quite another thing to say that all methods are and should be *equally* valuable. Again, it is one thing to say that a number of paradigms exist, and quite another to say that people who are located in one box cannot really understand the people in other boxes.

3 It is possible to make a distinction between what might be termed *attitude* pluralism and *doctrinal* pluralism. In the first sense, pluralism can be taken as representing a revival of spirited eclecticism. Pluralism in this sense is generous open-mindedness, and a resistance to intellectual closure. As Nicholas Rescher has wittily quipped, this is 'a Will Rogers kind of pluralism that never

met a position it didn't like'.[35] However, affable eclectic pluralism works *against* doctrinal statements of pluralism. In the latter,
monisms are simply to be ruled out as dangerous illusions; the
world and our ideas about it are multiple, not singular. End of
story.

4   The pluralism/monism encounter is intersected by at least two
    other controversial and mutually intertwined philosophical de-
    bates. The first is that around *realism* and *anti-realism*, and the
    second is the vexed issue of *relativism* versus *objectivism*. Now
    there is a common assumption, particularly in postmodernist
    writings, that methodological pluralism strictly implies both
    relativism and anti-realism, in the sense that reality is understood
    as discursively constructed. Moreover, the trend in critical social
    theory is to see this package of terms and positions as being both
    interesting and progressive. My commentary in this chapter has
    sought to problematize that chain of reasoning. Pluralism comes
    in various expressions and strengths, and the stronger varieties
    generate serious dilemmas. As a result, though sometimes set up
    as an independent methodological stance, pluralism often
    emerges as a secondary modifier within more familiar philosophi-
    cal options.[36] As in other fields, in metatheory pluralism seems at
    first sight to add something important, and seems to offer a new
    way forward. Unfortunately, perhaps, on reflection things turn
    out to be more complicated.

6
Radical Sociopolitical Pluralism

I

Frequently, a wide gulf is perceived to exist between the epistemo-logical/methodological level of discussion typical of the last chapter, and that of political description and advocacy. According to that perception, exercises in conceptual generality are sometimes considered 'merely abstract' and even 'elitist', whereas the depiction of 'concrete' political events and movements is said (often favourably) to be more 'accessible' and 'relevant'. Lately, though, this distinction, and its familiar polemical repertoire, has been scrambled to an unusual extent, as the whole realm of debate in the human sciences about what knowledge *is* (epistemology/methodology) has become inextricably bound up with debates about who and what knowledge is *for* (politics). Accordingly, methodology and metatheory have become considerably more politicized, whilst discussions of politics have become more abstract. Certainly, ideas about postmodern pluralist *politics* – the topic of this chapter – do not strike a very different note from that of postmodernist theoretical reflection generally. Rather, what we find is a continued attempt to investigate the nature of our many social identities today; to reconceive 'the social' and 'the political' pluralistically; and to witness the impact of that reorientation in thought upon our erstwhile assumptions about the purpose and fabric of political *action* – especially perhaps on the Left. The following statements capture the new radical pluralist mood.

The postmodern political condition is premissed on the acceptance of
the plurality of cultures and discourses. Pluralism (of various kinds)
is implicit in postmodernity as a project.[1]

At the heart of a postmodern culture is the acceptance of the
irreducible pluralistic character of social experiences, identities and
standards of truth, moral rightness, and beauty.[2]

Distinctive features of the new cultural politics of difference are to
trash the monological and homogeneous in the name of diversity,
multiplicity and heterogeneity; to reject the abstract, general and
universal in the light of the concrete, specific and particular; and to
historicize, contextualize and pluralize by highlighting the contingent, provisional, variable, tentative, shifting and changing.[3]

The new cultural politics of difference, the politics of diversity,
the politics of identity, radical democracy, the new republicanism,
the new social movements, subaltern empowerment, lifestyle
politics, lifeworld politics: these signature phrases recur time and
again in the postmodernist, post-Marxist, post-colonialist and
post-feminist literature, signalling the centrality of sociopolitical
pluralism to these critical discourses. In this discussion, I want to
consider the precise nature and implications of the new radical
pluralism, suggesting both the vitality of this movement, and
drawing attention to some serious dilemmas confronting it. These
problems are brought out by posing the following questions. In
what sense, exactly, is the new pluralism 'radical'? In what sense is it
'democratic'?

II

The new pluralism has emerged out of profound disenchantment
with structuralist and rationalist conceptions of society and politics.
More than anyone ever imagined in the 60s and 70s, it is plausible
now to argue that mainstream capitalist life and thought actually
shares with its long-standing opponent, Marxism, many central
'modernist' assumptions and tendencies. Moreover, some think
that these common features outweigh whatever continues to divide
the two world-views. The belief in societal centralism, in rational
progress, in a homogeneous public, in economic determinism, in a
Eurocentric cultural horizon, in psychic and sexual conservatism, in
social engineering have come to seem to the new radical pluralists

not only utterly questionable politically, but also wholly inadequate to the fabric of the societies in which we live.

It is not just that there has been a historical 'distortion' or two of Marx's (or anyone else's) true revolutionary vision, and that this distortion can be 'corrected' somehow by injecting the socialist project with a larger dose of humanism, liberal democracy, Trotsky, worker's control, or whatever. From a postmodernist radical perspective, the entire mind-set and *modus operandi* of the modern Left tradition as a whole is felt to be in need of dramatic replacement. The collapse of Soviet-style communism in the late 1980s was thus not simply the political failure of a particular socialist variant; it was a veritable social revolution *for* sociocultural pluralism itself, an overdue world historic assertion of social dynamism and complexity against the rigidity of industrial collectivism and moral policing.

Part of the thrust of this disaffection is to suggest that rationalist–collectivist alternatives to capitalism got history and society badly wrong. Instead of increasing social homogeneity and class consciousness, we have actually witnessed across the globe increasing diversity in material conditions, political aspirations and moral reference points. Instead of expecting and planning for one extraordinary crisis in the social fabric, governed by underlying structural-economic 'laws', we need to get attuned to the idea that a whole range of local and micro crises are experienced and negotiated frequently and ordinarily. Instead of 'society' being assumed to be the model set by the advanced western nations, we need to see that the rest of the world has steadfastly refused to be 'assimilated' into this model. In fact, the very fabric of life and culture in the metropolitan centres has been extraordinarily transformed by the growing presence of non-western 'others'. Also, instead of the information and technological revolutions heralding a monolithic brave new world of surveillance and control (of whatever ideological hue), 'post-Fordist' communications processes have simultaneously opened up opportunities for endless information-sharing and free association on the superhighway of devolved expertise.

Part of the problem, then, seems to be that monistic versions of socialism/Marxism have proved to be simply mistaken. That kind of critical judgement is probably *too* simple however, and in any case has been around for as long as Marxism itself. What is more specifically postmodernist in tenor is the view that 'society' is not the

kind of totalized 'object' that is open to accurate representation or
strategic manipulation – it is not any kind of object at all.[4]
Rationalist schemes of social mastery and fulfilment in that sense
are almost destined from the start to be dangerous misconceptions.
Theories and strategies are just not the sort of things that get things
right or wrong. Rather, postmodern pluralism accepts from the
outset that political theories and strategies are *constructed imagin-*
ary horizons, in the light of which we strive to make our collective
and individual identities. These are not 'mimetic' activities, as
implied by political rationalism, but rather 'affective' and sometimes unconscious processes of stabilization and disruption.

   In recognition that, necessarily, there will always be alternative
'social imaginaries' upon which to draw, and that our identifications
and responses will inevitably tend to be murky and incomplete, the
pluralism of postmodernism centrally involves acknowledging the
power of those unconscious and *non-rational* currents in which we
attempt to chart our life course. As a result, the concept of
'ideology', which has been so pivotal to all the rationalist political
schemes of modernity as a tool of analysis and rectitude, is placed
under erasure in postmodernist pluralism.[5] Instead of basing our
political views on a strict residual contrast between objective
knowledge and ideological misrecognition, a wide variety of
cognitive and subterranean imaginings are available for us to draw
on, and our political interests and personal self-images will be
constructed along the lines of their intersection. This means that, in
principle anyway, there is no more political 'correctness' as laid
down by the one true theory of social structure; there are only more
or less plausible, more or less persuasive standpoints, depending on
how it, and you, are positioned. Another far-reaching consequence
follows from this reversal of Enlightenment tenets. Just like
theories, programmes and movements, our individual *selves* are to
be regarded as radically plural phenomena in the postmodern
condition. A politics suited to the new era will thus have to be
geared to personal as well as political multiplicity.

III

The above sketch of postmodern pluralism is something of an ideal
type, but there is no shortage of writers who take the somewhat
abstract 'manifesto' just described as a guide for political thinking.

So it would be inappropriate to discount the postmodernist part of radical pluralism as a colourful backcloth only. After all, the keynote phrase, 'the politics of difference', gets its punch from its relationship of dependence/rejection with an equally strongly implied 'politics of sameness'. The logic of this is that the politics of difference notion emerges as being a more suitable plural outlook and strategy than the supposed monism of modernist Left politics. Most obviously in this genre, the Marxist focus on socioeconomic class as the single defining feature of past society and present politics is paradigmatically taken to represent the politics of sameness.

According to the latter, in class societies, and particularly in contemporary capitalism, the vast majority of people have in common, whether they know it or not, a certain (exploited) condition and an ultimate (emancipatory) interest. Furthermore, if we think and act collectively as revolutionary class-conscious agents for change, we will achieve a new, altogether better, but still *shared* condition and *shared* experience, namely that of an emancipated, wholesome, classless society in which our labour becomes for the first time a collective source of self-recognition, well-being and creativity.

Exponents of the politics of difference want to challenge this construction of our past ills and future release. What if there is no obvious political 'we' at all? What if our class condition is not shared or felt to be shared? What if class politics excludes, say, women and people of colour due to its formation in the historically male labour movement and in the heartlands of western industrial, imperialist culture? And what if that projected emancipated wholesomeness, with its continuing focus on the labouring human subject, is felt – from different points of view – to be culturally constricting and morally strait-laced? Such critical questions, even if left hanging only as questions, are sufficient to undermine some of the latent monistic assumptions of 'modernist radicalism',[6] particularly its Marxist variants.

The first major problem with postmodernist radicalism that I want to explore concerns the way in which it declares its departure from past orthodoxies. In this regard there is some tension between the two sorts of criticism of modernistic monism that I have outlined so far. On the one hand, there is the criterion of adequacy, which generates a kind of moral or empirical 'refutation' of the modernist–Marxist theory of politics. On the other hand, there is the suggestion that very different social imaginaries *always* exist, none of which is somehow 'truer' than the others. A tension arises here because this second criterion implies that refutation on the grounds of empirical or moral 'adequacy' (the first criterion) is actually impossible, since in such ideologically charged debate, there is simply no right or wrong about it. That is, we are really dealing with incommensurable *visions*. Two recent postmodernist pluralist texts illustrate this difficulty.

Anna Yeatman, for example, states that the very idea of a rational society 'free from domination has lost all credibility',[7] and Steven Seidman argues similarly that political appeals to human nature, reason, or the moral law simply 'lack moral credibility'.[8] Such criticisms of monistic modernism lead us to expect that by contrast postmodernist pluralism will be *more* credible. But take the following statements:

> Foundationalist epistemologies actively legitimate the bid for power of the New Class, and deeply implicate it in the modern, Western, state-centric, imperialist and capitalist system of domination.[9]

> The towering grandeur of scientific reason has all but crumbled under a barrage of assault from those who claim to be its victims: people of colour, non-Westerners, women, lesbians, and gay men, the disabled, and the poor and economically disempowered.[10]

It is not obvious from the texts how we are being asked to read these propositions. On the one hand, some empirical claims do seem to be being asserted; the tradition of scientific reason has come into question, there has been a broad movement of resistance against modernist styles of oppression, some new social strata are benefiting, and so on. On the other hand, the language is so stilted, and the claims so obviously contestable, that empirical 'credibility' as such barely comes into it. Rather, the statements are probably best seen as metonymic campaigns of rectification, statements of hope rather than of fact. Thus a dramaturgical villain is portrayed (Scientific Reason as the Great Excluder, the New Class as power-hungry Beneficiary of modernity), against whom the various heroes of the discourse band together. In other words, true to the postmodernist emphasis on the politics of rhetoric, a straight 'realist' reading of these statements is probably inappropriate. If that is so, however, then by the same token a realist assessment of modernist radicalism on the grounds of its apparent lack of credibility would also have to be forsaken.

IV

Perhaps because of the way in which such texts as those cited over-invest in the pronounced rhetoric of postmodernism, some people on the new-new Left prefer to see the politics of difference as representing a struggle and entanglement with modernist radicalism rather than as an across-the-board alternative. In taking this engaged stance, such writings are keenly aware of a range of further difficulties that the politics of difference needs to address.

1 One well-aired problem is the paradox that although themes of pluralism and rich multiplicity have been revived in order to counteract the uniform greyness with which modernist radicalism portrayed its recruits, the new pluralism can lead to a 'flatness' all of its own.[11] This depthlessness can emerge in the kind of postmodern philosophizing in which the principle of difference or multiplicity turns into just another ontological or methodological 'absolute', a new all-purpose privileged abstraction.[12] Instead of everything always being assumed to reveal an underlying, integrated logic of totality and integration, everything is now forever to be conceived as necessarily multiple, separate and differentiated. It could be argued, however, that this kind of position is just another type of monism – with a pluralist face.

2 In sociological terms, once all 'privileged' schemes of social classification have been questioned, the descriptive list of groups that appear to have a legitimate claim to separate mention becomes almost endless. The contemporary pluralist jigsaw thus contains pieces not only taken from Marxism (class formations), and corporatism (peak functional associations) and conventional pluralism (vocal, organized citizen pressure groups), but comprises in addition a huge array of lifestyle, consumption-based, belief-based, subcultural sources of personal identification. Moreover, many of these processes of identification occur in relation to media representations and simulations,[13] and this feature further underlines the feeling that it is simply impossible to put a definitive 'fix' on the relevant range of pluralist differentiation. A descriptive vastness ensues, a bland and thin egalitarianism of concerns, in which a myriad micro-situations have a rightful claim to full representation in the sociocultural matrix.

3 Against those philosophical and sociological backdrops, there is the tangible prospect that the politics of difference gradually blurs into the politics of *indifference*.[14] If there are very many legitimate interests and voices to be heard, and no dominant 'metanarrative', then each expression of autonomy is in effect as valid as any other. This is a severe problem for Leftists in particular, because under the newly risen pluralist sun, ironically, there seems to be a place for televangelists as well as trade unionists, for rugby clubs as well as women's groups, for paedophile rings as well as men's groups, and for white supremacists as well as anti-racists.

4 The balance of *individualism* and *collectivism* in the new pluralism has remained unresolved. Some regard pluralism as coming out of the liberal democratic tradition, and as referring centrally to 'the respect for individual rights'.[15] Nowadays, of course, the politics of individual rights and citizenship has turned into a complex and fruitful political arena for radicals, often undermining the legitimacy of the liberal regime in which those rights first emerged. Consequently, on the Left too, individualism gets a high profile. Accordingly, whilst group identities and interests are certainly important, they are not perceived as rigidly fixed any more. Rather, one thrust of the new politics is to see individual citizens or subjectivities as being situated, and situating themselves, between a multiplicity of different social identities and constituencies. In this picture, the rigid collectivist notions of identity and behaviour that defined the culture of the old Left, and led to moralistic expectations about political allegiances and behaviour, is abandoned.

Yet in some ways to bring out the 'radical' potential of pluralism, its connection with the individualism of liberalism must be decisively cut. The whole thrust of early pluralist thought, for example, was emphatically to *reject* liberal individualism, because it encouraged free-riding, and worked against group identities and functional representation. So the balance between group and individual constructions, between moralism and free-riding, is a precarious one. Above all, radicals could be expected to strongly reject an individualist–relativist approach to identity – the 'I'm OK, you're OK' syndrome.[16] Antipathy to such complacency still exists, for sure, but it is no longer clear that there is any firm theoretical basis for it.

In this context, and in the light of the noticeable lack of *institutional* proposals amongst the radical theorists of difference, one strand of thinking attempts to establish a viable *associative* democracy for the present day.[17] This position seeks to chart a course between the poles of 'the state' and 'individuals' by reasserting the primacy of group identity, and by seeing corporate organization as an essential feature of modern society. The basic claim is that the shape of the democratic polity needs to be moulded around associational self-government in all spheres of life. In this model, there is no intention of underestimating the fundamental importance of the central state; the state has a vital role to play in creating the umbrella structures and enforcement agencies of the plural society. At the same time, once that democratic and enabling framework is in place, it is possible to envisage a very considerable downloading of resources and capacities to the level of the associations. The resourcing structure of the associative commonwealth will no doubt encourage organizations to form themselves along the enduring fault lines of society (types of work role, consumption profiles, communities of belief and ethnic identification, neighbourhood functions, cultural expression, etc.), and to be themselves internally ordered in a democratic way. There is no necessity for the latter, however, as long as no harm is done to the wider community. Although the primacy of group life is stressed, organizationally speaking, the modern sensitivity to individualism is there too, since associations are conceived as definitively *voluntary* in membership and motivation.

A full exposition and appraisal of associative democracy is not appropriate in the present discussion. Nor am I advocating this line as such. It may well be, for example, that, when considered in terms of its coordination across multiple geographical, economic and social contexts, associationalism runs right into all the old problems of political centralism versus devolution, of the authority of the state versus that of individuals, of socialist 'planning' as against the more fluid pluralism of market-driven difference. But even so, associationalism is a refreshing and concrete recipe for achieving civic responsibility without social uniformity, and mutualism without communalism.

5 Pluralism is not necessarily of the Left, but through the 1980s it seemed that sociopolitical pluralism could be given a distinctly

'progressive' coloration through the idea of the *new social movements* (NSMs). These movements – green politics, black politics, the politics of disability, feminism, the peace movement, the grey movement, youth movements, and so on – were imagined as partly standing against the outdated and somewhat imperialistic politics of the labour movement, but in another way they were also seen as carrying forward from labourism and revolutionary socialism the baton of radical progress.

This analysis, whilst highly attractive for a period, has run out of steam to an extent. For one thing, although the NSM label seemed 'structural' enough to act as a successor category to class, its sociological rationale is hard to make out. In one sense, the NSMs that are most frequently referenced have a very clear class location: in the professional *petit bourgeoisie*. In another sense, though, the very notion of social *movements* undercuts traditional 'structural' sociological analysis. This is because it is the element of value-commitment rather than social location that is central to the logic of the NSMs; they are very much 'elective communities'.[18]

Given the first two problems, a third arises. Why is it that only *progressive* elective communities are typically included as component NSMs within the politics of difference?[19] For example, perhaps the most striking social movement today is *nationalism*, which is a classic combination of chosen, ascribed and inherited elements of social identity. But of course, the latter's political connotations are not always progressive in the eyes of many on the old and new Left, and so nationalism seldom appears on lists of 'approved' NSMs.

The sense in which the NSMs are *unified* movements – indeed the sense in which they are 'movements' at all – is also somewhat problematical. This is partly because the new politics sometimes has a deliberately unorganized character – some movements are more in the way of cultural phenomena rather than organized politics, whilst others seek to break the mould of traditional organized politics altogether. They develop and congeal through informal networks rather than in or through centralized political parties. As a result, however, sometimes the talk about the existence of NSMs is unaccompanied by very much coordinated action.

Additionally, it is important to note that a marked process of pluralization has occurred over the years within many of the NSMs; we speak today of feminisms rather than feminism, of the politics of peoples of colour rather than black politics, and so on. Finally we should note that NSMs can come and go, leaving the question of enduring or umbrella *values* still pertinent after a particular *cause* has been won or lost. For example, mainstream politics has gradually taken on board some of the rhetoric and demands of the NSMs, reducing both their novelty and distinctiveness; NSMs might also simply lose momentum, perhaps through ineffective strategies, or through the failure of spokespeople to be representative of their supposed constituencies, or through changing world circumstances (for example the peace movement in a post-Cold War era). All in all, the attractive image of the 1980s – that there were really only a handful of new social movements, and that these were both progressive and here to stay for some considerable time – has become rather more complicated in the 1990s.

V

Theorizing on the nature of *identity* and *subjectivity* is perhaps the most innovative aspect of the new cultural politics of difference. The latter's typical strengths, but also some of the problems already mentioned, can readily be seen in considering what radical pluralism involves in this area.

Potentially, radical pluralism encompasses two divergent projections of identity politics. One of these, in direct contrast to translocational constructions of our concretely experienced identifications, leads to a kind of local essentialism. For example, the idea of making the authentic voice of marginalized and oppressed groups heard; the idea that no one from outside a particular group can speak on its behalf; the notion of fundamentally distinct black or women's or physically challenged interests and history; the invocation of a collective political Other to counteract the suppositions of western 'orientalist' ideology – these sorts of ideas summon up a kind of 'separate spheres' pluralism which holds great potential not only for the expression of resilience and solidarity under pressure, but also for autochthonous mythologies and sectarianism.

An alternative way of conceptualizing the politics of identity would be to see social subjectivity in the (post)modern world as increasingly traversing particular subcultures, social locations and value stances. Instead of assuming identities as being fixed according to *either* some global principle *or* some local group formation, identities can be viewed as being formed and re-formed at the intersections of, and in the interstices between, different socio-political discourses. From this angle, identity formation, and thus identity politics, is the process of negotiating and articulating *hybridity*. In particular, attention has been paid to the way in which, both historically and in the current scene, western metropolitan cultures (together with standard countercultures of the Left) have from the start been entangled with, and enabled by, the cultural politics of the black diaspora.[20]

Generalizing the insights of this line of scholarship, it would appear to be unproductive to speak of singular and 'given' socio-cultural identities – whether 'black' or 'western'. At the same time, any route from here to the easy 'I'm OK, you're OK' approach to political negotiation is firmly blocked. Rather, 'hybridity' represents a version of identity politics which strives to understand the social sources of affective belongingness, but does not hesitate to draw attention to the ideological and conservative dimensions of this crucial cultural phenomenon. Rather like deconstruction in cultural theory, upon which it draws, hybridity analysis is thus concerned to unsettle any attempt to set up a prearranged harmony between social positions and moral-political stances.[21]

The analysis of 'hybridity' has been developed primarily in relation to the experience of diaspora, and of post-colonial migration more generally, but the notion of cultures of hybridity would seem to have a wider applicability. Thus, Stuart Hall writes: 'Cultures of hybridity are one of the distinctly novel types of identity produced in the era of late-modernity, and there are more and more examples of them to be discovered.'[22] This is because hybrid cultures are constituted by the process of experiential and symbolic *translation* of older cultural touchstones within newly situated groups and individuals.[23] Now, we might add here that whilst this experience of cultural syncretism is particularly acute and particularly interesting in the diaspora, it is also a growing characteristic of the cultures and subcultures of 'the West' itself. Postmodern social differentiation, increasing exposure to world news, an increasingly comparative and reflexive public consciousness, and the everyday witnessing of the crumbling of the historic colonial empires and values are notable tendencies which arguably produce a similarly complex, hybrid spread of identities and interests in the social core of industrial modernity itself. This is now an essential part of the pluralist fabric of life and politics in the 'advanced' societies.

Along these lines, the pluralist philosopher Michael Walzer has nicely drawn attention, after the Chinese manner, to the 'four great mobilities' of life in modern societies.[24] Walzer argues that the effect of the pronounced processes of geographical, marital, social and political mobility is to bind radical pluralist projects to an essentially *liberal* world-view, however much radicals might wish to resist this. Of course, some theorists of hybridity would wish to see themselves as remaining 'oppositional' in a key sense, but Walzer's point is that the terms of that opposition to mainstream liberalism are now much more nuanced, less dramatically polarized, given the relentless pluralization of previously solid reference points for revolutionaries.

The politics and theoretical basis of the focus on hybrid identities in cultural analysis is thus somewhat ambiguous – and consciously so. It is not clear, for example, whether 'hybridity' is intended to complement or to refute the thesis that societies in our epoch have become profoundly globalized. Taken one way, hybridity is the sign of increasing social and political complexity – a move precisely away from the uniformity of past times. Under another lens, though, it can be argued that it is not so much *actual* social complexity/ plurality that has dramatically increased, but rather simply our *awareness* of difference. Indeed, this shared awareness of plurality is one of the chief cultural products of the historically unprecedented spread of *common* discourses, economic imperatives and communication channels at a world level. In this reading, the universality of the language of quasi-democratic political ideologies, the relentless drive to nationhood amongst peoples, the movement towards globally compatible communications systems, the commodification of the lifeworld, the 'McDonaldization' of youth culture, the reach of multinational firms, and so on, are the signs and syndromes of long-term cultural convergence, not differentiation *per se*. A major issue around pluralism then, is whether the underlying pattern in global social terms lends support to the idea of 'one world' or, in direct contrast, to the idea of 'many worlds'.[25] Whilst it would be misleading to think of cultural hybridity theory as categorically linked to the 'many worlds' thesis as against 'one worldism', there is considerable need for further elaboration on this issue.

Another consequential matter which remains unresolved is the extent to which hybridity is intended to be a prescriptive as well as an analytical-descriptive concept. There are grounds for thinking that it is intended as the new preferred way of being, if only because it directly undercuts the moral weight of all 'essentialist' appeals, whether local or global in character. The hybrid cultural predicament then emerges as something of a model for the (post)modern pluralist consciousness, wrestling with the issue of how to live awkwardly (but also wisely and critically) in the midst of a number of strong value stances and historical formations.[26]

There are some drawbacks here, though. Currently, the experience of hybridity and reflection upon it is most obvious amongst radical intellectual circles. By an obvious twist of fate, these intellectual communities tend to be sophisticated, urban and upwardly mobile, and it simply might not be the case that the majority of people outside those subcultures experience anything like the plurality of identities, or the feeling of excitement/ contradiction that plurality creates in that environment.[27] More generally, the feeling of cultural and social dislocation as often turns people *towards* essentialist symbolic strategies as towards syncretic modes of expression. The postmodern 'migrancy' authors[28] perhaps dismiss this phenomenon too swiftly, at least normatively speaking. The felt need for social belongingness clearly runs very deep, and by comparison the ironic cast of the rootless consciousness would not seem to be conducive to the establishment of enduring or distinctive cultural reference points. Hybridity, in other words, does not easily produce a *people*. Meanwhile, there is an echo, in some discussions of hybridity, of earlier attempts to build a 'postideological' culture around the socially detached, but socially concerned, intelligentsia.[29]

VI

Up to now, the question of the *democratic* import of the new pluralism has been implicit in much of the discussion, but it has not been openly tackled. I want to do that now. Above all, I want to re-emphasize and examine the proposal that social pluralism is intrinsic to contemporary proposals for 'radical democracy'.

In reaction to Left monism, and drawing on apparently richer theoretical resources, notably the writings of Gramsci, pluralistically inclined Marxists and socialists have attempted to retain something of the overall aims and terminology of socialism, but have loudly insisted that formal democracy and societal pluralism are absolutely central, rather than incidental, to the radical project. Of particular importance here is the notion of 'civil society', that complex realm of social intercourse, group formation and moral–political action which is theorized as being (ordinarily) both ungoverned by the formal institutions of the state and also irreducible to the logic of the dominant (capitalist) mode of production. In that vein, it has been widely asserted that if socialist ideas are to be rejuvenated, and indeed if a socialist future is to be desirable at all, then civil society must be recognized and positively promoted as *the* vital social arena, characterized in its very nature by cultural pluralism and democratic impulses. Thus one prominent 'civil society' author states that socialism must become 'a synonym for greater democracy – for a differentiated and pluralistic system of power'.[30]

Other radical pluralists have doubted whether socialism actually adds anything useful or achievable to pluralism and democracy. They have drawn attention to the fact that, not only in traditional Marxist–Leninist conceptions of history and politics, but in Gramsci too, and perhaps in *any* conception of socialism as a distinct social goal, a holistic and oppressive telos is necessarily at work. That telos or 'social imaginary' inevitably, and not merely incidentally, flattens out social plurality and pushes our sense of democratic reconstruction into something like the old homogenizing mould. In that sense, even 'civil society' socialists, arguably, are not in fact taking pluralism as the very 'starting point' for analysis and advocacy.[31] The point here would be that radical democracy should be taken as a successor paradigm to socialism, and not merely pictured as one of the latter's preconditions.

This sharp revision of the Left's starting point and goal is very challenging, since traditional socialism and social democracy as well as orthodox Marxism/Communism are as a consequence put into serious question as being surplus to requirements. Put another way, even if pluralism and democracy are taken to be *necessary* conditions for socialism, it is hard to see how they can supply the *sufficient* conditions in any meaningful sense.[32] This is because socialism involves, over and above pluralism and democracy, a conception of justice as substantive equality, the primacy of the human values of mutuality and cooperation, and the thesis that the character of the total collectivity, and especially its organization of human labour, profoundly shapes the nature and benefits of individual and group lives. Yet it is just those 'added' dimensions that are now perceived as contestable. For that reason, radical democratic pluralism seems to its supporters to be a leaner, more attractive and also a more feasible theoretical option for post-modern times.

What can be said in qualification of radical pluralist democracy as the banner of the new Left? One perhaps surprising comment is that it is not self-evident, nor can it be guaranteed in advance, that radical pluralism *is* necessarily 'democratic'. I have been arguing throughout this book that pluralism is best understood as the acceptance of social and intellectual diversity. However, at some point the emphasis on diversity runs right against the 'imaginary presuppositions' of democracy itself.[33] To elaborate: although there may well be a plurality of social constituencies in the demos, according to the very language of radical democratic thought, the demos must still be posited as *collectively* participating in an ethically and socially fulfilling process of *self-government*. The assumption of all democratic theory is thus that the different component groups of a society are constituted as a 'people', and it is *as* a people that they come to a relatively harmonious consensus about their collective destiny. The contemporary thrust of post-modern radical pluralism, by contrast, is to put into jeopardy such totalizing notions as 'the people'.

In some ways, the most suitable ironic way to take democracy is to see it as a limited decision-making procedure within liberal societies. It might even be appropriately regarded as simply an ideology of 'consultation' deployed by basically authoritarian governments. In addition, probably the most consistent under-standing of democratic decision-making, namely rule by the people as a whole, expressed operationally as *majority* rule, may involve denying the kind of group autonomy and sovereignty that pluralists espouse. We might also note that democracy, in just about any of its variations, is a quintessentially *representational* notion, in that the situational characteristics and value agenda of a social body are conceived as being represented and expressed within a more circumscribed domain, the polity. Once again, though, the firmly anti-representational inclination of postmodernism would seem to counsel against associating pluralism with democracy in that regard.

The unexpected upshot of these considerations is that in spite of its searing critique of old-guard socialism, radical pluralism can only be connected to a conception of popular democracy by playing up its continuity with classic Left concerns. For all its scepticism about them, the radical democratic pluralist scenario actually requires two defining features of modernist radicalism, namely *normative collectivism* and *methodological holism*. Without these governing tropes, there is nothing very radical (in the political sense) about pluralism at all, and yet with them we are immediately thrown into the kind of 'surplus' social imaginary that postmodernist theory suspects.

The final dilemma of radical pluralism I want to touch upon is an extension of this last observation. Postmodern radicals counsel us to give up on totalizing 'imaginaries' as a guide to progressive politics. But how then does radical democratic pluralism differ from the common liberal–pluralist recommendation of institutional pragmatism? Accepting that all types of 'surplus' principles or ascriptions must be regarded as coercive, Steven Seidman for one implores progressive analysts to see that:

> a pragmatic approach to knowledge that assumes that there is no neutral agency to resolve differences and that we must struggle, case by case, to negotiate identities, norms and common understandings promotes a beneficent pluralism and democracy.[34]

In similar fashion, Anna Yeatman asserts that the democratic politics of difference 'requires this post-ontological type of political community to commit itself to certain kinds of proceduralism'.[35]

These sorts of claim imply a purely procedural and piecemeal approach to the process of democratic expression. No doubt this approach has its merits when highlighted against the background of strong revulsion from 'essentialist' social and political theory.[36] Yet at the same time, it is hard to see how any coherent general analysis can emerge from such a firmly pragmatist and proceduralist basis. This aspect of the politics of difference also runs the risk of deep inconsistency, in that whilst macro-level images of society and politics are rigorously purged of generic essences and surplus hopes, the 'authenticity' of group identities at the micro-level, and their 'transparent' expression in political negotiation, gets rather taken for granted.

Not only that, the business of deciding what constitutes, in Seidman's words, 'beneficent' pluralism as against 'destructive' pluralism, and how the former is going to be policed in the widest sense, are not directly addressed by radical pragmatism. Pluralists of any kind are always faced with a decision about where to draw the line. You *can* be an 'ultra-pluralist', of course, in which case you do not draw lines; anything goes, in politics as in theory. The plurality in this case is literally endless and unpoliceable. On the whole, though, this form of pluralism, in spite of its great consistency and challenge, has not proved to be popular. Indeed, the political and methodological literature is awash with texts which assert the need for pluralism to *avoid* nihilism and ultra-relativism almost as much as foundationalism, statism and so on. In that case, however, you cannot escape developing an account of the legitimate range of plural groups and outlooks, and how it is going to be enforced in the real world of people and ideas. One of the most serious flaws in postmodernist pluralist writings is that these questions tend to be evaded.

A strong postmodernist politics of difference, then, with its relentless deconstruction and its effective pragmatism, in some ways leaves us without 'principled positions' of a substantive kind.[37] Unhappy with this consequence, Left-inclined commentators are attempting to try once again to achieve an integrated combination of pluralism and universalism. High on the wish list here is the possibility that *radical pluralism* might turn out in the end to be pretty much the same thing as *radical humanism*.[38] There remains some prevarication in the face of this impulse, because the very label 'humanism' (however 'radical' we make it sound) has been the target of more than three decades of structuralist and poststructuralist polemic.

Nevertheless, we seem to have reached the end of that particular polemical line. The truth is that whilst the effect of pluralism and deconstruction on critical thinking has been fascinating and indelible, these currents have not as yet proved effective for positive moral and political reconstruction. Accordingly, various tentative rescue operations are under way, in which old-style notions of solidarity, community, responsibility for others, togetherness, care, and so on, are being built into the respect for plurality and difference.[39] Serving as a powerful protest against Left political 'guardianship' and static, tainted images of the (male, white, working) 'people', the trumpeting of 'difference' has been perceived to hit some odd notes. The fear is that we may be embarked upon an uncontrollable process of 'splitting' – within the Left, within each radical subculture, within each organizational forum, and even within our individual selves – to the point where all remnants of the various 'emancipatory' projects are obliterated.

VII

Let me close by turning head-on to the question of how much the new cultural politics of difference differs from conventional pluralism. Given the discussion of this chapter and earlier ones, we can say overall that, terminological differences aside, some of the older pluralist observations and goals have been rediscovered by radicals as if they were entirely fresh. In tandem, the utter confidence shown by 1970s radicals in structuralist and emancipatory motifs for critique has seriously weakened. True, conventional pluralism is not the same as it was either; it has moved to the left. On balance, however, it has perhaps burned fewer of its boats, and you can see this by comparing two important books by Robert Dahl and Iris Young.[40]

In *Democracy and Its Critics* (1989), Dahl seems to be in a less obviously 'critical' mood than he was in the early 1980s, returning to the concept and practical merits of 'polyarchy' in the liberal democracies (free and fair elections, inclusive suffrage, associational autonomy, accountability of political élites). Certainly, Dahl freely admits that polyarchy is only a *necessary* and by no means a *sufficient* condition for adequate democracy. Indeed, Dahl reveals his raised consciousness by acknowledging that the tradition of polyarchy in the USA was founded specifically as 'white male polyarchy'.[41] At the same time, he counsels vigorously against uncompromising radical alternatives, whether these centre around notions of rigorous equality, or the common good, or the general will, or the idea of wholly 'principled' political conduct, or emancipation, or 'full' participatory democracy.

Dahl also elegantly reformulates his sociological baseline. Its centrepiece is the concept of a society which is modern, dynamic and pluralist (MDP). For Dahl, whilst there is no necessary tie-up between the MDP society and even polyarchy, never mind some fuller expression of democracy, the MDP indisputably exists today as the predominant 'advanced' social form, and furthermore only an MDP society, in his view, can provide the material for enlightened democratic progress. That society is characterized by political inclusiveness, cultural complexity, urban patterns of interaction and affiliation, a predominantly market economy, and yet also a relatively wide dispersal of wealth, education, power and authority across its component subcultures.[42]

Iris Young, in *Justice and the Politics of Difference* (1990), periodically attempts to distance her own pluralist inclinations from those of the 'interest group pluralists' amongst whose number Dahl is often counted. This attempt misfires in key respects however. Most notably, Young characterizes conventional pluralists as being overly individualistic in their sense of group membership, and guilty of presenting group identities as private, self-regarding behaviour. However, this underestimates Dahl's long-standing commitment to public control of the political agenda, and his conception of group politics as emerging not out of sectional bargaining *per se*, but from the character of societal subcultures. Even David Truman, in the inaugural text of post-war American pluralism, constructed something of a metaphysics of group being in an effort to assert the deep human significance of the various pressure group interests.[43] Similarly, when Young urges radicals to accept group differentiation as being desirable as well as inevitable, and when she writes of that process as 'multiple, cross-cutting, fluid, and shifting', her phraseology is extraordinarily reminiscent of routine conventional pluralist formulas.[44]

There are other marked coincidences. For example, both Young and Dahl pay specific, deadly attention to the harm caused by the transcendental notion of the 'common good', and in that vein they each take the now familiar pot-shot at the dystopian 'Rousseauist dream' of egalitarian homogeneity. Both our exemplars are perfectly 'at home' in the cool (post)modern metropolitan milieu, and they share a basic criterion of democracy as the right of all those who are affected by a major decision to be involved in prior deliberation around it. At the same time, Young and Dahl are quick draw attention to the dangers inherent in deep subcultural pluralism: dissonance, strife and the militant assertion of essentialist identities. They also agree that the solution to these problems lies in building a robust civic culture of pragmatic cooperation; a politics of mutual respect for autonomy and difference; and (in spite of their conjoint scepticism about the common good) an overarching commitment amongst the citizenry to the sort of umbrella polity that can sustain and foster diversity without rancour. On balance, Young advocates group representation in the polity more firmly than Dahl does, but both are rather hesitant to pronounce on this, and are certainly at one in seeing liberal individualism in any strict sense as unsatisfactory. Yet it is equally true that in the MDP today, the importance of individual autonomy renders the process of group differentiation and affiliation a complex and irreducible matter.[45]

There are of course differences between conventional pluralism and the politics of difference. My point is simply but importantly that these differences are not as dramatic as is often made out, and are becoming less noticeable with the passage of time. Thus Young insists on seeing some significant differences between groups as constituting oppression, a category which includes elements of economic exploitation, cultural imperialism, and violence. Dahl is less 'structuralist' and less radical, though he too views the source of political inequalities as lying in 'differences in resources and opportunities for employing violent coercion; in economic positions, resources and opportunities; and in knowledge, information and cognitive skills'.[46] Here Dahl *does* show a distinctly sharper awareness of undesirable 'difference' than was apparent in mainstream pluralism 30 years ago. But still, it is interesting that it is, in the end, the residual *non-pluralist* elements of the radical perspective – its structuralism, rationalism and its dual 'essentialist' motif of oppression/emancipation – that finally distances Young's treatment of the new politics of difference from Dahl's overview of pluralist democracy's pasts and prospects.

7

Conclusion: Pluralism Revised

In Chapter 1, I set out the overall goals of this study, and to a large extent prefigured its conclusions too. That being so, I will simply revise the main themes of the book in the form of the following 'theses on pluralism'.

1 The force of any brand of pluralism depends on its ability to characterize and problematize some prevailing monistic orthodoxy. In that sense, pluralism is a 'generic' concept, an intellectual congeries or syndrome, rather than a fixed paradigm or specific tradition. The precise connotations and implications of pluralism thus vary according to era and intellectual domain.

2 The general concept of pluralism divides into three distinct but interrelated levels of abstraction: the methodological, the sociocultural, and the political. Within these categories, further subdivisions are possible. Unless we are aware of this matrix of meanings, overarching talk of pluralism will be of limited value.

3 In most contexts of discussion, the pluralist impulse generates three core dilemmas. The first lies in deciding whether or not pluralism, in qualifying the 'big pictures', itself then constitutes a new 'big picture'. 'Strong' pluralism, for example, militantly opposes *all* single-minded perspectives, but in doing so tends to result either in ironic scepticism or in an equally single-minded particularism. Alternatively, 'moderate' pluralism strives only to insist that we regard the various militant positions as constituting a menu of options, not as exclusive dogmas. In that case, however, pluralism remains parasitic upon the vitality of monistic world-views.

4 The second constitutive dilemma of pluralism is the problem of how to impose principled limits on the proliferation of acceptable entities, theories, and political formations that are unleashed by strong forms of pluralism.

5 The third dilemma is whether or not *descriptive* pluralism must involve *prescriptive* pluralism. On the face of it, a commitment to portray whatever social and methodological diversity exists should not inevitably lead to the affirmation of plurality as a good thing. In that case, plurality does not entail pluralism. However, recent movements in epistemology tell us that we usually find what we are looking for, and so our very 'recognition' of diversity *does* often imply temperamental and ideological pluralism.

6 We are all pluralists now. If the monism–pluralism encounter is about as close as you get to an eternal configuration of human dialogue, a glacial shift away from monism, towards pluralism has occurred over time. Where once the onus was on pluralists to bounce off, and to try to dismantle, the grand monistic edifices, today any credible 'big picture', will have to be very careful not to appear to obliterate or devalue perceived plurality.

7 Methodological and political pluralism lie at the heart of what is most interesting about postmodernism and postmodernity. Dilemma, ambivalence, paradox: the new pluralism seems to shape up as a significant way of addressing and even resolving in a progressive way the typical agonism of the postmodern predicament. It is better to regard pluralism as a more tangible name *for* that very predicament, however.

8 Late modernity/postmodernity in liberal bourgeois–democratic society is characterized by pluralism not only in theory, but in everyday life too. Civil society today contains a great many ideas and mechanisms for managing issues about who we are, what we believe in, and about which groups are to be included as our equals and fellow citizens. Is there just one right view of things, events, and the good life – or many? This question is the touchstone of contemporary philosophizing about pluralism, but it also emerges, unmodified, out of our contemporary social experience.

9 More than its advocates are willing to concede, the new cultural politics of difference revivifies ideas that were already present in conventional political pluralism. The latter is accordingly owed an apology for the sometimes shabby way it gets treated by radicals.

10 Radical–democratic pluralism does not, however, completely converge with liberal and pragmatist pluralism. This is because it preserves some familiar socialist and humanist (and therefore 'universalist') goals. Some people feel uneasy about this persistent element of traditionalism, but it remains morally and analytically vital. It is morally important because pragmatic pluralism is devoid of inspiration at a time when, as a species, we badly need mutualist inspiration. It is analytically important too, because although the pluralistic obsession with difference has an attractive purchase in terms of immediate experience, it can become myopic. Critical social science, and radical humanist politics thus cannot do without the kind of longer term, evolutionary point of view that inevitably stands as a counterpoint to deconstructive pluralism.

11 The most institutionally consequential aspect of radical political pluralism is the notion of *associational* organization and representation. This contribution cuts between statism and individualism, without entirely forsaking those established horizons. However, the institutional viability of 'associative democracy' has not yet been established in any decisive way. That is only the most concrete sense in which the transformative capacity of pluralism, even now, remains to be seen.

Notes

Chapter 1

1 This transformation will be noted again as we proceed. For an account, see G. McLennan, *Marxism, Pluralism and Beyond* (Cambridge: Polity Press, 1992) Ch. 2; also J. Manley, 'Neo-Pluralism: A Class Analysis of Pluralism I and Pluralism II', *American Political Science Review*, 77(2) 1983.

2 See the references to the 'new' philosophy of social science in Chapter 4. Classically, it has been thought that, above all, we need theories to *explain* events, patterns and processes. Across the philosophy of natural and social science, however, there is some debate about just what explanation means. See for example P. Achinstein, *The Concept of Explanation* (Oxford: Oxford University Press, 1983).

3 C.O. Schrag, *The Resources of Rationality: A Response to the Postmodern Challenge* (Bloomington: Indiana University Press, 1992) p. 30. See also McLennan, *Marxism, Pluralism and Beyond*, Ch. 5. For a less reserved account along similar lines see K. McClure, 'On the Subject of Rights: Pluralism, Plurality and Political Identity', in C. Mouffe (ed.) *Dimensions of Radical Democracy: Pluralism, Citizenship, Community* (London: Verso, 1992).

4 C. Mouffe, 'Liberalism, Socialism and Pluralism: Which Citizenship?', in J. Squires (ed.) *Principled Positions: Postmodernism and the Rediscovery of Value* (London: Lawrence & Wishart, 1993) p. 69.

5 Other schemes for subdividing pluralism are proposed in R. Breitling, 'The Concept of Pluralism', in S. Ehrlich and G. Wooton (eds) *Three Faces of Pluralism* (London: Gower, 1980) and W. Watson, 'Types of Pluralism', *The Monist*, 73, 1990.

6 On dilemmatic thinking, see M. Billig, *Arguing and Thinking: A Rhetorical Approach to Social Psychology* (Cambridge: Cambridge University Press, 1987); M. Billig *et al.*, *Ideological Dilemmas: A Social Psychology of Everyday Thinking* (London: Sage, 1988).

Chapter 2

1 C.A. MacKinnon, *Toward a Feminist Theory of the State* (Cambridge, MA: Harvard University Press, 1989) p. 4.
2 Ibid., p. 11.
3 Ibid., p. xii.
4 E.M. Wood, *The Retreat from Class: A New 'True' Socialism* (London: Verso, 1986) p. 63.
5 M. Barrett and A. Phillips, 'Introduction', in M. Barrett and A. Phillips (eds) *Destabilizing Theory: Contemporary Feminist Debates* (Cambridge: Polity Press, 1992) p. 3.
6 Ibid., p. 4.
7 N. Fraser and L.J. Nicholson, 'Social Criticism without Philosophy: An Encounter between Feminist and Postmodernism', in L.J. Nicholson (ed.) *Feminism/Postmodernism* (New York and London: Routledge, 1990) pp. 34–5.
8 J. Flax, 'Postmodernism and Gender Relations in Feminist Theory', in L.J. Nicholson (ed.) *Feminism/Postmodernism*, p. 52.
9 Fraser and Nicholson, 'Social Criticism', p. 31.
10 L. Nicholson, 'Editor's Introduction', *Feminism/Postmodernism*, p. 2.
11 S. Harding, 'Feminism, Science and the Anti-Enlightenment Critiques', in *Feminism/Postmodernism*, pp. 96–7.
12 H.E. Longino, 'Subjects, Power and Knowledge: Description and Prescription in Feminist Philosophies of Science', in L. Alcoff and E. Porter (eds) *Feminist Epistemologies* (London: Routledge, 1993) p. 113.
13 R. Pringle and S. Watson, ' "Women's Interests" and the Post-structuralist State', in M. Barrett and A. Phillips, *Destabilizing Theory*, p. 65.
14 See C. Ramazanoglu, 'Introduction', in C. Ramazanoglu (ed.), *Up Against Foucault: Explorations of Some Tensions between Foucault and Feminism* (London: Routledge, 1993).
15 Pringle and Watson, ' "Women's Interests" ', p. 56.
16 Ibid. p. 56.
17 S. Walby, 'Post-Post-Modernism? Theorizing Social Complexity', in M. Barrett and A. Phillips, *Destabilizing Theory*, p. 31.
18 Pringle and Watson, ' "Women's Interests" ', p. 65.
19 Ibid., p. 69.
20 See e.g. D. Truman, *The Governmental Process* (New York: Alfred A. Knopf, 1951) p. 43; N.W. Polsby, *Community Power and Social Theory* (New Haven, CT: Yale University Press, 1963) p. 118.
21 G. Almond and S. Verba, *The Civic Culture: Political Attitudes and Democracy in Five Nations* (Boston, MA: Little Brown & Co., 1965). See also G. Almond and S. Verba (eds) *The Civic Culture Revisited* (Boston, MA: Little, Brown & Co., 1980).
22 Pringle and Watson, ' "Women's Interests" ', p. 67.

23 Ibid., p. 69.

24 Ibid., p. 63.

25 See e.g. D. Fuss, *Essentially Speaking: Feminism, Nature and Difference*, (New York and London: Routledge, 1989).

26 I.M. Young, 'The Ideal of Community and the Politics of Difference', in *Feminism/Postmodernism*, p. 301.

27 C. de Stephano, 'Dilemmas of Difference: Feminism, Modernity and Postmodernism', in *Feminism/Postmodernism*, p. 77.

28 S. Benhabib, 'Epistemologies of Postmodernism: A Rejoinder to Jean-Francois Lyotard', in *Feminism/Postmodernism*, p. 123–4.

29 Cited in L. Nicholson, 'Introduction', *Feminism/Postmodernism*, p. 7.

30 M. Barrett and A. Phillips, *Destabilizing Theory*, p. 6.

31 A. Phillips, 'Universal Pretensions in Political Thought', in *Destabilizing Theory*, p. 28.

32 M. Barrett and A. Phillips, *Destabilizing Theory*, p. 8.

33 Z. Bauman, *Modernity and Ambivalence* (Cambridge: Polity Press, 1991).

34 J. Flax, *Thinking Fragments: Psychoanalysis, Feminism, and Postmodernism in the Contemporary West* (Berkeley, CA: University of California Press, 1990) pp. 218–9, p. 233. See also R. Braidotti, *Nomadic Subjects* (New York: Columbia University Press, 1994), and P. Lather, *Getting Smart* (London: Routledge, 1991) for postmodernist-feminist authors who carry subjective hybridization and plural inclusiveness about as far as it will go ... *without* yet quite feeling comfortable about embracing relativism or abandoning the residual notion of 'emancipation'.

35 Harding, 'Feminism, Science and the Anti-Enlightenment Critiques', p. 86.

Chapter 3

1 B. Russell, *My Philosophical Development* (London: George Allen & Unwin, 1959) pp. 54–61.

2 B. Russell, 'The Philosophy of Logical Atomism', reprinted in D. Pears (ed.) *Russell's Logical Atomism* (London: Fontana, 1918/1972) pp. 59–60.

3 W. James, *A Pluralistic Universe* (Cambridge, MA: Harvard University Press, 1909/1977) p. 26.

4 Ibid. p. 63.

5 See e.g. B. Russell, *History of Western Philosophy* (London: George Allen & Unwin, 1948) Ch. 29.

6 James, *A Pluralistic Universe*, p. 32.

7 R.J. Bernstein, 'Introduction' to James, *A Pluralistic Universe*, pp. xxii–xxv.

8 Ibid., p. 141.

9 Ibid., p. 143.

10 J. Ward, *The Realm of Ends, or Pluralism and Theism* (Cambridge: Cambridge University Press, 1911) Lecture IX.

11 H.J. Laski, *Studies in the Problem of Sovereignty* (New Haven, CT: Yale University Press, 1917) p. 6.

12 Ibid., p. 1. Coincidentally, in *The Realm of Ends* (p. 185) Ward too used a political analogy, except that from his quasi-idealist angle of vision, the pluralist universe is said to resemble 'so many village communities without a supreme federation, geographically neighbours but strangers politically'.

13 H.J. Laski, *The Foundations of Sovereignty and Other Essays* (1921) as abridged in P.Q. Hirst (ed.) *The Pluralist Theory of the State: Selected Writings of G.D.H. Cole, J.N. Figgis, and H.J. Laski* (London: Routledge, 1989) p. 185.

14 On the New Liberalism, see S. Hall and B. Schwarz, 'State and Society, 1880–1930', in M. Langan and B. Schwarz (eds) *Crises in the British State* (London: Hutchinson, 1985).

15 F.W. Maitland, 'Introduction' to O. von Gierke, *Political Theories of the Middle Ages* (Cambridge: Cambridge University Press, 1988); B. Bosanquet, 'Introduction' to *The Philosophical Theory of the State*, 2nd edn (London: Macmillan, 1910) p. xxiii.

16 E. Barker, 'The Discredited State', *Political Quarterly*, 5 February, 1915.

17 A.W. Wright, *G.D.H. Cole and Socialist Democracy* (Oxford: Clarendon Press, 1979) p. 39.

18 G.D.H. Cole, *The Social Theory* (London: Methuen & Co., 1920); *Guild Socialism Re-Stated* (London: Leonard Parsons, 1920).

19 J.N. Figgis, *Churches in the Modern State* (London: Longman, Green & Co., 1913).

20 See P.Q. Hirst, 'Introduction' to *The Pluralist Theory of the State*; M. Walzer, *Spheres of Justice: A Defence of Pluralism and Equality* (Oxford: Martin Robertson, 1983); J. Matthews, *The Age of Democracy* (Melbourne: Oxford University Press, 1989); J. Cohen and J. Rogers, 'Associative Democracy', *Politics & Society* 20(4) 1992; P.Q. Hirst, *Associative Democracy: New Forms of Economic and Social Governance* (Cambridge: Polity Press, 1994).

21 The following account of both the conventional and critical pluralist paradigms draws on Chapter 2 of my *Marxism, Pluralism and Beyond* (Cambridge: Polity Press, 1989). Other useful summaries can be found in P. Dunleavy and B. O'Leary, *Theories of the State* (London: Macmillan, 1987) and D. Held, *Models of Democracy* (Cambridge: Polity Press, 1987).

22 G. Almond and S. Verba, *The Civic Culture: Political Attitudes and*

Democracy in Five Nations (Boston, MA: Little, Brown & Co., 1965).

23 Actually, a critical wing of political science pluralism was also around prior to the postwar version of the American Dream. See for example, E.E. Schattschneider, *Politics, Pressures and the Tariff* (New York: Prentice Hall, 1935).

24 See e.g. P. Schmitter and G. Lehmbruch (eds) *Trends Towards Corporatist Intermediation* (London: Sage, 1979); S. Berger (ed.) *Organizing Interests in Western Europe: Pluralism, Corporatism and the Transformation of Politics* (Cambridge: Cambridge University Press, 1981).

25 P. Schmitter, 'Neo-corporatism and the State', in W. Grant (ed.) *The Political Economy of Corporatism* (London: Macmillan, 1985) p. 55.

26 See e.g. L. Panitch, 'The Development of Corporatism in Liberal Democracies', in P. Schmitter and G. Lehmbruch, *Trends Towards Corporatist Intermediation*; O. Newman, *The Challenge of Corporatism* (London: Macmillan, 1981).

27 A. Cawson, *Corporatism and Political Theory* (Oxford: Blackwell, 1986) p. 6.

Chapter 4

1 M.G. Smith, 'Institutional and Political Conditions of Pluralism' and 'Some Developments in the Analytic Framework of Pluralism', in L. Kuper and M.G. Smith (eds) *Pluralism in Africa* (Berkeley, CA: University of California Press, 1969); also 'The Nature and Variety of Plural Units', in D. Maybury-Lewis (ed.) *The Prospects for Plural Societies* (Washington DC: American Ethnological Society, 1984).

2 J.S. Furnivall, *Colonial Policy and Practice* (Cambridge: Cambridge University Press, 1948).

3 L. Kuper and M.G. Smith, *Pluralism in Africa*; N. Rhoodie (ed.) *Intergroup Accommodation in Plural Societies* (Pretoria: Macmillan, 1978).

4 M.G. Smith, 'The Nature and Variety of Plural Units', pp. 160, 170–1.

5 Ibid., p. 153.

6 See e.g. J. Rex, *Race, Colonialism, and the City*, Part 4: 'Pluralism, Colonial Conflict and Black Revolution' (London: Macmillan, 1973).

7 See e.g. C. Clarke *et al.* (eds) *Geography and Ethnic Pluralism* (London: George Allen & Unwin, 1984); M. Keith and S. Pile (eds) *Place and the Politics of Identity* (London: Routledge, 1992).

8 For this and other important aspects of multicultural democracy see C. Taylor *et al.*, *Multiculturalism and 'the Politics of Recognition'* (Princeton, NJ: Princeton University Press, 1992).

9 See A. Lijphart, *Democracy in Plural Societies* (New Haven, CT: Yale University Press, 1977).

10 See J.G. Kellas, *The Politics of Nationalism and Ethnicity* (London: Macmillan 1991) Chs 9–11. My own understanding of these issues has been informed by the politics of biculturalism and multiculturalism in Aotearoa/New Zealand. See for example the special 'National Identities/Futures' issue of *Sites: A Journal for South Pacific Cultural Studies*, 30, 1995.

11 F.W. Maitland, 'Introduction' to O. von Gierke, *Political Theories of the Middle Ages* (Cambridge: Cambridge University Press, 1988).

12 E. Ehrlich, *Fundamental Principles of the Sociology of Law* (New York: Arno Press, 1913/1975; trans. 1936).

13 For the distinction between weak and strong legal pluralism, and generally for the best overview, see J. Griffiths, 'What is Legal Pluralism?', *Journal of Legal Pluralism*, 1. Also S.E. Merry, 'Legal Pluralism', *Law and Society Review*, 22, 1988.

14 P. Fitzpatrick, 'Law, Plurality and Underdevelopment', in D. Sugarman (ed.) *Legality, Ideology and the State* (London: Academic Press, 1983) p. 160.

15 This key phrase comes from S.F. Moore, *Law as Process: An Anthropological Approach* (London: Routledge and Kegan Paul, 1978).

16 See e.g. B.Z. Tamanaha, 'The Folly of the "Social Scientific" Concept of Legal Pluralism', *Journal of Law and Society*, 20(2) 1993.

17 B. de Sousa Santos, 'State, Law and Community in the World System: An Introduction', *Social and Legal Studies*, 1(2) 1992, p. 132.

18 For a postmodernist perspective on legal subjecthood, see for example, P. Goodrich, *Languages of Law: From Logics of Memory to Nomadic Masks* (London: Weidenfeld and Nicolson, 1990).

19 See B. Erlich, 'Amphibolies: On the Critical Self-contradictions of "Pluralism"', *Critical Inquiry*, 12(3) Spring 1986.

20 Followers of Richard McKeon's difficult, strenuous philosophical writings would probably challenge the way in which, like other commentators, I have passed him by in an attempt to get an easier fix on Chicago pluralism through its literary representatives. See J.E. Ford, 'Introduction' to special issue of *The Monist*, 73, 1990.

21 S. Pepper, *World Hypotheses: A Study in Evidence* (Berkeley, CA: University of California Press, 1942); H. White, *Metahistory: The Historical Imagination in Nineteenth Century Europe* (Baltimore, MD: Johns Hopkins University Press, 1973).

22 To the point where, in history too, postmodernism and pluralism have fused, throwing the discourse into some disarray. See e.g. K. Jenkins, *Re-thinking History* (London: Routledge, 1991).

23 W. Booth, *Critical Understanding: The Powers and Limits of Pluralism* (Chicago, IL: University of Chicago Press, 1979) p. 12.

24 Ibid., p. 32–3.
25 W. Booth, 'Pluralism in the Classroom', *Critical Inquiry*, 12(3) 1986, p. 479.
26 H. White, 'Historical Pluralism', *Critical Inquiry*, 12(3) 1986, p. 486.
27 See e.g. W. Conolly (ed.) *The Bias of Pluralism* (New York: Atherton Press, 1969).
28 W.J.T. Mitchell, 'Pluralism as Dogmatism', *Critical Inquiry*, 12(3) 1986, p. 498; Ehrlich, 'Amphibolies', p. 524; E. Rooney, *Seductive Reasoning: Pluralism as the Problematic of Contemporary Literary Theory* (Ithaca, NY: Cornell University Press, 1989, pp. 17–18.
29 Rooney, *Seductive Reasoning*, p. 3.

Chapter 5

1 C. Hempel, *Aspects of Scientific Explanation* (New York: The Free Press, 1965).
2 K. Popper, *Conjectures and Refutations* (London: Routledge and Kegan Paul, 1965); T.S. Kuhn, *The Structure of Scientific Revolutions* (Chicago, IL: University of Chicago Press, 1962); I. Lakatos, *The Methodology of Scientific Research Programmes* (Cambridge: Cambridge University Press, 1979); L. Laudan, *Progress and Its Problems: Towards a Theory of Scientific Growth* (London: Routledge and Kegan Paul, 1977); R. Bhaskar, *A Realist Theory of Science* (Brighton: Harvester Press, 1978).
3 K. Popper, 'The Myth of the Framework', in E. Freeman (ed.) *The Abdication of Philosophy* (La Salle, IL: Open Court, 1976); also, *Objective Knowledge* (Oxford: Clarendon Press, 1972).
4 See e.g. B. Barnes and D. Bloor, 'Relativism, Rationalism and the Sociology of Knowledge', in M. Hollis and S. Lukes (eds) *Rationality and Relativism* (Oxford: Blackwell, 1982).
5 D. Thomas, *Naturalism and Social Science: A Post-Empiricist Philosophy of Social Science* (Cambridge: Cambridge University Press, 1979).
6 H. Putnam, *Reason, Truth and History* (Cambridge: Cambridge University Press, 1981) pp. 73–4; H. Putnam, *Realism and Reason* (Cambridge: Cambridge University Press, 1983) p. 183; P. Feyerabend, *Farewell to Reason* (London: Verso, 1987) p. 77; N. Goodman and C.Z. Elgin, *Reconceptions in Philosophy* (London: Routledge, 1988) p. 53.
7 See e.g. P. Achinstein, *The Concept of Explanation* (Cambridge: Cambridge University Press, 1983).
8 This has been one of the key themes in Richard Rorty's pragmatist style of pluralism. See his *Consequences of Pragmatism* (Brighton: Harvester Press, 1982) and *Contingency, Irony, Solidarity* (Cambridge: Cambridge University Press, 1989).

9 See A. Pickering (ed.) *Science as Practice and Culture* (Chicago, IL: University of Chicago Press, 1992).

10 P. Diesing, *How Does Social Science Work?: Reflections on Practice* (Pittsburgh, PA: Pittsburgh Press, 1991) p. 321.

11 Ibid., p. 364.

12 J. Bohman, *The New Philosophy of Social Science* (Cambridge, MA: MIT Press, 1991) p. 233.

13 Ibid., p. 232.

14 P.A. Roth, *Meaning and Method in the Social Sciences: A Case for Methodological Pluralism* (Ithaca, NY: Cornell University Press, 1987) p. 5.

15 See Z. Bauman, *Modernity and Ambivalence* (Cambridge: Polity Press, 1991); S. Harding, *Whose Science? Whose Knowledge?* (Milton Keynes: Open University Press, 1991); A. McRobbie, 'New Times in Cultural Studies', *New Formations*, 13 (Spring) 1991, pp. 1–18.

16 See L. Grossberg *et al.*, *Cultural Studies* (London: Routledge, 1992) pp. 1–2; F. Inglis, *Cultural Studies* (Oxford: Blackwell, 1993) p. 227.

17 See S. Hall, 'Cultural Studies and the Centre: Some Problematics and Problems', in S. Hall *et al.* (eds) *Culture, Media, Language* (London: Hutchinson, 1980).

18 D. Hebdige, *Hiding in the Light* (London: Comedia/Routledge, 1988) Ch. 7; A. McRobbie, 'Post-Modernism and Cultural Studies', in L. Grossberg *et al.*, *Cultural Studies*.

19 J. Alexander, 'The Centrality of the Classics', in A. Giddens and J. Turner (eds) *Social Theory Today* (Cambridge: Polity Press, 1987).

20 See e.g. N. Mouzelis, *Back to Sociological Theory* (London: Macmillan, 1992); A. Gurnah and A. Scott, *The Uncertain Science: Criticism of Sociological Formalism* (London: Routledge, 1992).

21 D. Weinstein and M.A. Weinstein, 'The Postmodern Discourse of Metatheory', in G. Ritzer (ed.) *Metatheorizing* (Newbury Park, CA: Sage, 1992) p. 140.

22 D.W. Fiske and R.A. Schweder, 'Editors' Introduction: Uneasy Social Science', *Metatheory in Social Science: Pluralisms and Subjectivities* (Chicago, IL: University of Chicago Press, 1986) p. 1.

23 J.C. Alexander, *Theoretical Logic in Sociology*, Vol. 1 (London: Routledge and Kegan Paul, 1982) p. 66ff. Also J.C. Alexander and P. Colomy, 'Traditions and Competition: Preface to a Postpositivist Approach to Knowledge Cumulation', in G. Ritzer (ed.) *Metatheorizing*.

24 For a useful discussion of political and epistemic issues in methodology, see M. Hammersley, *Social Research: Philosophy, Politics and Practice* (London: Sage, 1993).

25 H. Siegel, *Relativism Refuted* (Dordrecht: Reidel, 1987) p. 163.

26 R.A. Schweder, 'Divergent Rationalities', in D.W. Fiske and R.A. Schweder, *Metatheory in Social Science*.

27 See R. Bhaskar, *Scientific Realism and Human Emancipation* (London: Verso, 1987).

28 C. Geertz, 'Anti-Anti-Relativism', *American Anthropologist*, 86, 1984.

29 E. Gellner, *Postmodernism, Reason and Religion* (London: Routledge, 1992) p. 55.

30 Ibid., p. 60.

31 P.-M. Rosenau, *Post-Modernism and the Social Sciences* (Princeton, NJ: Princeton University Press, 1992) p. 119.

32 N. Goodman, *Ways of Worldmaking* (Indianapolis, IN: Hackett Publishing Co., 1978).

33 See e.g. H. Siegel, *Relativism Refuted*, p. 159; also N. Rescher, *Pluralism: Against the Demand for Consensus* (Oxford: Clarendon Press, 1993) p. 73.

34 See R. Sylvan, 'Radical Pluralism – An Alternative to Realism, Anti-realism and Relativism', in R. Nola (ed.) *Relativism and Realism in Science* (Dordrecht/Boston/London: Kluwer Academic, 1988).

35 N. Rescher, *Pluralism*, pp. 90–91.

36 Thus, for example, Siegel's position is a kind of pluralistic 'absolutism' (in *Relativism Refuted*, p. 163); Reschers position makes pluralism compatible with both 'empiricism' and 'rationalism', *Pluralism*, pp. 78, 101; whilst Feyerabend's position amounts to a fully committed 'relativism', *Farewell to Reason*, Ch. 1.

Chapter 6

1 A. Heller and F. Feher, *The Postmodern Political Condition* (Cambridge: Polity Press, 1988) p. 5.

2 S. Seidman, *Contested Knowledge: Social Theory in the Postmodern Era* (Oxford: Blackwell, 1994) p. 324.

3 C. West, 'The New Cultural Politics of Difference', in C. West, *Keeping Faith: Philosophy and Race in America* (New York: Routledge, 1993) p. 3.

4 E. Laclau, 'The Impossibility of Society', in E. Laclau, *New Reflections on the Revolution of Our Times* (London: Verso, 1990).

5 This move is often less decisive than it appears, with 'demystification' prominent as a substitute category. See e.g. M. Barrett, *The Politics of Truth* (Cambridge: Polity Press, 1991) p. 167; and C. West, *Keeping Faith*, p. 23.

6 S. Crook, *Modernist Radicalism and Its Aftermath* (London: Routledge, 1991).

7 A. Yeatman, *Postmodern Revisionings of the Political* (London: Routledge, 1994, p. 7)

8 S. Seidman, *Contested Knowledge*, p. 191.

9 A. Yeatman, *Postmodern Revisionings*, p. 40.

10 S. Seidman, *Contested Knowledge*, p. 327.

11 L. Marcil-Lacoste, 'The Paradoxes of Pluralism', in C. Mouffe (ed.) *Dimensions of Radical Democracy: Pluralism, Citizenship, Community* (London: Verso, 1992) p. 131.

12 S. Crook, *Modernist Radicalism*, p. 173; C.O. Schrag, *The Resources of Rationality* (Bloomington, IN: Indiana University Press, 1992) p. 32; C. Ramazanoglu, 'Introduction', in C. Ramazanoglu (ed.) *Up Against Foucault* (London: Routledge, 1993) p. 10.

13 K. Thompson, 'Social Pluralism and Postmodernity', in S. Hall *et al.* (eds) *Modernity and its Futures* (Cambridge: Polity Press, 1992) p. 251.

14 C. Mouffe, 'Democratic Politics Today', in *Dimensions of Radical Democracy: Pluralism, Citizenship, Community* (London: Verso, 1992) p. 13.

15 C. Mouffe, 'A Radical Left Project?', in S. Wilks (ed.) *Talking About Tomorrow* (London: Pluto Press, 1993) p. 70.

16 C. Calhoun, 'Social Theory and the Politics of Identity', in C. Calhoun (ed.) *Social Theory and the Politics of Identity* (Oxford: Blackwell, 1994) p. 24.

17 Notably P.Q. Hirst, *Associative Democracy: New Forms of Economic and Social Governance* (Cambridge: Polity Press, 1994).

18 See e.g. A. Touraine, 'Is Sociology Still the Study of Society?', *Thesis Eleven*, 23, 1989; and A. Giddens, *Modernity and Self-Identity: Self and Society in the Late Modern Age* (Cambridge: Polity Press, 1991) Ch. 7.

19 This happens even in good summaries of the new social movements, e.g. S. Crook *et al.*, *Postmodernization: Change in Advanced Society* (Newbury Park, CA: Sage, 1992) Ch. 5.

20 P. Gilroy, *The Black Atlantic: Modernity and Double Consciousness* (Cambridge, MA: Harvard University Press, 1993).

21 S. Hall, 'Cultural Identity and Diaspora', in J. Rutherford (ed.) *Identity* (London: Lawrence & Wishart, 1990).

22 S. Hall, 'The Question of Cultural Identity', in S. Hall *et al.* (eds) *Modernity and Its Futures*, p. 310.

23 See H.K. Bhabha, 'Introduction', in H.K. Bhabha (ed.) *Narrating the Nation* (London: Routledge, 1990); K. Robins, 'Tradition and Translation: National Culture in its Global Context', in J. Corner and S. Harvey (eds) *Enterprise and Heritage: Crosscurrents of National Culture* (London: Routledge, 1991).

24 M. Walzer, 'The Communitarian Critique of Liberalism', *Political Theory*, 18(1) 1990, pp. 11–12.

25 See M. Archer, 'Sociology for One World: Unity and Diversity', *International Sociology*, 6(2) 1992, and subsequent debate in that journal.

26 For interesting moral theorizing on pluralism as navigating a wise pathway between monism and relativism, see J. Kekes, *The Morality of Pluralism* (Princeton, NJ: Princeton University Press, 1993).

27 C. West, *Keeping Faith*, pp. 27–8.

28 See e.g. I. Chambers, *Migrancy, Culture and Identity* (London: Routledge/Comedia, 1994); and R. Braidotti, *Nomadic Subjects* (New York: Columbia University Press, 1994).

29 K. Mannheim, *Ideology and Utopia* (London: Routledge and Kegan Paul, 1936); D. Bell, *The End of Ideology* (New York: The Free Press, 1962).

30 J. Keane, *Democracy and Civil Society* (London: Verso, 1988) p.3.

31 E. Laclau and C. Mouffe, *Hegemony and Socialist Strategy* (London: Verso, 1985; p.140); see also E. Laclau, *New Reflections*, and M. Walzer, 'The Civil Society Argument' in C. Mouffe (ed.) *Dimensions of Radical Democracy: Pluralism, Citizenship, Community* (London: Verso, 1992).

32 See L. Martell, 'New Ideas of Socialism', *Economy and Society*, 21(2) 1992.

33 B. Hindess, 'Imaginary Presuppositions of Democracy', *Economy and Society*, 20(2) 1991.

34 S. Seidman, *Contested Knowledge*, p.278.

35 A. Yeatman, *Postmodern Revisionings*, p.89. For a 'conflict management' pluralism, see A.O. Hirschman, 'Social Conflicts as Pillars of Democratic Market Society', *Political Theory*, 22(2) 1994.

36 But see M. Nussbaum, 'Human Functioning and Social Justice: In Defence of Aristotelian Essentialism', *Political Theory*, 20(2) 1992.

37 J. Squires (ed.) *Principled Positions: Postmodernism and the Rediscovery of Value* (London: Lawrence & Wishart, 1993).

38 J. Weeks, 'Rediscovering Values', in J. Squires (ed.) *Principled Positions*, p.195.

39 Ibid.; I.M. Young, 'Togetherness in Difference', in J. Squires, *Principled Positions*; S.K. White, *Political Theory and Postmodernism* (Cambridge: Cambridge University Press, 1991) p.137f.

40 R.A. Dahl, *Democracy and Its Critics* (New Haven, CT: Yale University Press, 1989); I.M. Young, *Justice and the Politics of Difference* (Princeton, NJ: Princeton University Press, 1990).

41 R.A. Dahl, *Democracy*, pp.221–2, 253.

42 Ibid., pp.251–2.

43 I.M. Young, *Justice*, pp.114–6, 186, 190–1; R.A. Dahl, *Democracy*, pp.254–5; D. Truman, *The Governmental Process*, (New York: Alfred A. Knopf, 1951) p.505.

44 I.M. Young, *Justice*, pp.47–48; and, for example, D. Truman, *The Governmental Process*, p.43.

45 For this sequence of points, compare I.M. Young, *Justice*, pp.119, 230, 236–7, 91, 169, 186–9, 184, 172–3, with R.A. Dahl, *Democracy*, pp.282ff, 294, 251, 306, 255, 341, 297, 112.

46 Young, *Justice*, p.50ff.; Dahl, *Democracy*, p.323–4.

Select Bibliography

Introductory

Ehrlich, S. and Wootton, G. (eds.) (1980) *Three Faces of Pluralism: Political, Ethnic and Religious*. London: Gower.
Nichols, D. (1974) *Three Varieties of Pluralism*. London: Macmillan.

General

McLennan, G. (1989) *Marxism, Pluralism and Beyond*. Cambridge: Polity Press.

Feminism and Pluralism

Nicholson, L. (ed.) (1990) *Feminism/Postmodernism*. New York: Routledge.

Associational Pluralism

Hirst, P.Q. (ed.) (1989) *The Pluralist Theory of the State: Selected Writings of G.D.H. Cole, J.N.Figgis, and H.J.Laski*. London: Routledge.
Hirst, P.Q. (1993) *Associative Democracy: New Forms of Economic and Social Governance*. Cambridge: Polity Press.

Conventional/Critical Pluralism

Berger, S. (ed.) (1981) *Organizing Interests in Western Europe: Pluralism, Corporatism and the Transformation of Politics*. Cambridge: Cambridge University Press.
Dahl, R.A. (1989) *Democracy and its Critics*. New Haven, CT: Yale University Press.

The Plural Society

Kuper, L. and Smith, M.G. (eds.) (1969) *Pluralism in Africa*. Berkeley, CA: University of California Press.

Legal Pluralism

Griffiths, J. (1986) 'What is Legal Pluralism?' *Journal of Legal Pluralism*, 24: 1–55.

Interpretative Pluralism

Booth, W. (1979) *Critical Understanding: The Powers and Limits of Pluralism*. Chicago, IL: University of Chicago Press.
Critical Inquiry, (1986) 12(3) special issue on 'Pluralism and Its Discontents'.

Methodological and Epistemological Pluralism

Fiske, D.W. and Schweder, R.A. (eds.) (1986) *Metatheory in Social Science: Pluralisms and Subjectivities*. Chicago, IL: University of Chicago Press.
Monist (1990) 73, issue on 'Systematic Pluralism'.
Rescher, N. (1993) *Pluralism: Against the Demand for Consensus*. Oxford: Clarendon Press.

Pluralism and the Politics of Difference

Mouffe, C. (ed.) (1992) *Dimensions of Radical Democracy: Pluralism, Citizenship, Community*. London: Verso.
Young, I.M. (1990) *Justice and the Politics of Difference*. Princeton, NJ: Princeton University Press.

Moral Pluralism

Kekes, J. (1993) *The Morality of Pluralism*. Princeton, NJ: Princeton University Press.
Walzer, M. (1993) *Spheres of Justice: A Defence of Pluralism and Equality*. Oxford: Martin Robertson.

Index